CYBERSLAMMED

understand | prevent | combat | transform
the most common cyberbullying tactics

A Curriculum Workbook With

Strategic Advice for Middle and High School Students

Kay Stephens & Vinitha Nair

sMASHUP PRESS

This workbook was made possible by the generous support of Time Warner Cable

ISBN-13: 978-0-615-64180-5
LCCN: 2012910137

Printed in the United States of America

Contents

APPENDICES

Acknowledgments

Over the last twenty years, each of us has been a mentor and educator to tweens and teens, both in urban and rural environments and in privileged and at-risk settings. As friends and colleagues, we have years of working with kids in educational programs and have shared a common goal to help teenagers navigate an ever-changing, online landscape. Though the framework of this workbook was our own design, we needed expert advice to provide educators and parents with a hands-on resource that dealt with specific cyberbullying situations. For that, we turned to a number of educators, authors, law enforcement, legal experts, and bully/cyberbully experts for their advice, including:

- Mike Donlin, the Senior Program Consultant for the Seattle Public Schools' "Middle School Cyberbullying Curriculum," who helpfully lent examples of Seattle, Washington's cyberbullying policy;

- Maine's Cyber Crime Unit and the Maine Attorney General's Office for their legal expertise;

- Thomas Hutton, an attorney with the Seattle, Washington law firm Patterson, Buchanan, Fobes, Leitch, and Kalzer, and a former in-house counsel with the National School Boards Association, reviewed all of the workbook's "Threat Assessment" sections, providing valuable advice for parents and teachers on how to react appropriately and when to bring in law enforcement or consider civil or criminal lawsuits;

- Lyn Mikel Brown, Ed.D., author of *Girlfighting: Betrayal and Rejection Among Girls*, provided feedback and insight on relational aggression in our "Digital Pile On" chapter;

- Jayne Hitchcock, author and internationally recognized cyber crime expert, lent oversight to our Sexting chapter;

- Joshua Herman, an attorney at Miller, Hall & Triggs, LLC in Peoria, Illinois, also reviewed the particular legal issues within our Sexting chapter. Herman prosecutes for local governments, focuses on educational and governmental law, and has published analysis and guidance regarding various Sexting issues;

- Shanterra McBride, Founder/Director of Preparing Leaders of Today, examined the "Haters' Club" chapter and gave some practical advice for real-life consequences;

- Chuck C. Nguyen, a martial artist/bullying expert, translated Eastern philosophies of resilience and self-defense into compassionate advice for students who have been emotionally injured in the "Transform" section of each chapter;
- Stan Davis, co-author with Charisse Nixon, PhD, of The Youth Voice Research Project, also provided advice in the "Transform" section on how to overcome peer mistreatment;
- Anne Collier, the co-author of *MySpace Unraveled: A Parents' Guide to Teen Social Networking* and *A Parents' Guide to Facebook*, was incredibly generous with her time on this project. She helped us refine the entire tone of the introductory sections of this workbook;
- Nancy Willard, MS, JD, executive director of the Center for Safe and Responsible Internet Use and author of *Cyberbullying Legislation and School Policies*, provided a number of insights in this workbook around Sexting as well as parental/school responsibilities in cyberbullying situations.

We'd like to thank the Maine Girls Collaborative Project for their support in the research phase of this workbook and especially to our sponsor, Time Warner Cable for their generous support in the publication of this workbook. Thanks also go to Maggi Blue and Tabitha Lowe for design consultation, BJ Bowden, a school counselor at MSAD 41 of Milo, Maine for educator feedback, and Dianne Fields, a Massachusetts educator and an integral part of our focus group process. Waynflete Academy in Portland, Maine and the Women's Resource Center at the University of Maine in Orono, Maine provided us the location and time to do a test drive of this material with their middle school students.

On a personal note, Kay thanks her family for their support around the origins that spurred the creation this workbook—particularly her mother, for exploring strategic solutions to help embattled targets regain their power. She is grateful to Vini Nair for not only being a great friend, but for being just as willing to see the whole project through on days when prize cow dramas, and real life seemed to get in the way of the dream.

Vini would like to thank her family and friends. Their support was indispensable in launching her budding nonprofit venture, which helped frame the research behind this workbook. She would also like to thank her husband for riding this rollercoaster with her, as well as Kay for reminding her that one's impact is not always in how many kids are served; it can be just as significant and rewarding as helping even one person through a difficult time.

Introduction

Imagine being a teenager today and clicking on a link to see a web page dedicated entirely to ridiculing you. Not just a web page—but hundreds of comments from people you may or may not know passing judgment on you for entertainment value, lying about your character, or saying things like: "Everybody hates you" or, "Why don't you just die?"

The suicide of a 13-year-old girl named Megan Meier who'd been cyberbullied in 2006 was a large part of the reason this workbook came to be; it prompted us to research the correlation of cyberbullying incidents to the drastic choices victimized teens sometimes make in these situations.[1]

At the time the media reported Meier's story nationally there weren't even proper terms invented yet for the Imposter Profile that had been used against her. Reporters tried to define it as a "cruel cyber hoax" and "a fictitious profile," yet many adults unfamiliar with social media didn't understand what these terms really meant.[2]

The media also drew a direct connection between the pain Meier suffered at the hands of her cyberbullies and her death. The thought that a fake MySpace profile could cause a young girl to take her life horrified millions of Americans. With every new high-profile case in the news, a stronger correlation was made in the public perception that cyberbullying was the direct cause of teen suicide. Yet, as experts in suicide prevention caution, not every case is the same and it's important that we don't draw overly simplistic and inaccurate conclusions. Though suicide is an extremely rare response to social aggression, a combination of factors create the condition for suicide, such as what the teen's relationships are like at school and at home, as well as how resilient or how vulnerable he or she is to setbacks and blows.[3]

That said, when Megan Meier's story hit the news, like most people, we were appalled to discover that a calculating adult was behind the impersonation and that many of Meier's peers were willing bystanders. Her case compelled us to find out what kinds of tactics played a part in cyberbullying and what parents and school administrators could do to prevent this from happening to another teen.

According to a 2010 national study by the Chicago youth-market research firm TRU, nearly one third of US teens report some sort of online bullying, defamation, and harassment.[4] A 2011 MTV/Associated Press study suggests that cyberbullying among teens ages fourteen to twenty-four has become a pervasive problem of modern adolescence. According to the study, seventy-six percent of these teens say digital abuse is a serious problem for people their age, with fifty-six percent reporting that they have experienced abuse through social and digital media.[5] The study additionally pinpoints the most common targets of online harassment and discrimination tend to be students who are overweight, female, African-American, immigrants or who are lesbian, gay, bisexual or transgender.[6] Authors and co-directors of the Cyberbullying Research Center, Dr. Justin W. Patchin and Dr. Sameer Hinduja, found that the most commonly reported cyberbullying tactics include posting mean or hurtful comments and spreading rumors online, with girls more likely to be the ones spreading rumors while boys are more likely to post hurtful pictures or videos[7]. The 2011 MTV/AP Study also found that typical tactics included: people writing things online that were mean and untrue and people forwarding an IM or message that was intended to stay private.[8]

With every tragic news story involving cyberbullying, the public's fear and anger ratcheted up. Who was responsible for this? How do we stop it? Cyberbullying itself seemed like such an amorphous, broad concept. What is it exactly? Just when parents, educators, and prosecutors began to grasp what it was, *it* kept changing. With each new technological application that gained popularity (social networking, texting, micro blogging, iPods) the tactics of cyberbullying mutated. Even people vaguely familiar with the concept of cyberbullying understood that in the wrong hands, everyday social technology could have disastrous consequences.

In the early 2000s, we had the perfect incubator to observe patterns of cyberbullying. Within Platform Shoes Forum (PSF), a nonprofit organization that develops digital learning networks, we both worked with a national community of middle school girls through Zoey's Room, PSF's online program that encouraged their interest in science, technology, engineering, and math (STEM) careers. As excited as the girls in our clubs were to communicate electronically, there was a flip side. It was inevitable that conflict offline had the potential to include online blowups and cyber snipes here and there. That's when we started to witness the full spectrum of disruptive online behaviors—from one-time incidents to repeated intentional aggression. Quickly, we created protocols to address these types of issues, and when the girls learned which online behaviors were expected of them, cyberbullying incidents drastically decreased.

In response to a parental and school demand, we were the first in Maine to offer a series of Internet Safety and cyberbullying prevention workshops. Our home state was already a pioneer in the area of increasing access to digital technology in schools. With its ground-breaking learning technology initiative in 2000, Maine led the 1-1 computing movement that offered free laptops to every middle and high school student from 7th to 12th grade in order to give them access to the type of twenty-first century skills they'd need to be competitive in future careers.[9]

However, as many parents attested in our workshops, despite each school's "Acceptable Use" policy around using these laptops, many students did not receive any formal training on how to behave ethically online. Students were instructed not to "harass" anyone online without actually knowing what specifically constituted harassment. It was a familiar problem, as we, too, created a digital learning network that initially had no cyberbullying guidelines. More than a decade later, most schools have learned what we learned. Handing students a laptop for schoolwork has all the best intentions, but when teens are not prepared to understand the consequences (legal or otherwise) of online derision and defamation, technology becomes a dangerous tool.

Around the time we started doing statewide workshops, Kay Stephens wrote a young adult novel titled *Ethel Is Hot (LOL)*, about a 12-year-old girl cyberbullied by her entire school. *Cyberslammed* intended to be a companion educator workbook to the novel, explaining how some of the tactics worked. This workbook took on an even larger scope when Vinitha Nair, the Co-founder and Executive Director of Platform Shoes Forum, joined as co-author.

For the next four years, we researched the most common tactics of cyberbullying, many of which were pulled from national headlines. We particularly looked to the latest insights from Anne Collier's blog, NetFamilyNews.org, along with Sameer Hinduja and Justin W. Patchin's excellent resource: *Bullying Beyond The Schoolyard.*

In our research phase, with the help of Maine Girls Collaborative Project, we conducted more than a dozen focus groups throughout New England, working with middle and high school students to drill down even farther and focus on six specific tactics. *Cyberslammed* takes into account that a student can one day be a cyberbully, but another day be the target of one, so we looked at each tactic from various perspectives—the bully, the target, the bystander, as well as the ally. One of our primary goals is to encourage schools to require and enact policies around cyberbullying prevention as well as implement measured processes to handle incidents and consequences. Another goal of this workbook is to separate the behavior from the technology. Thus, we added a conflict resolution exercise to each corresponding chapter in order to encourage students to express empathy/responsibility for targets of cyberbullying and identify their roles as allies, not perpetrators.

Our intent with *Cyberslammed: Understand, Prevent, Combat, And Transform The Most Common Cyberbullying Tactics,* is to help decrease incidents of cyberbullying by encouraging self-protection in digital environments, informing both educators and students about what constitutes potential criminal activity, as well as increasing public awareness and promoting ethical behavior online.

Overview

Let's imagine for a moment you are an educator observing one of your students in a martial arts class. She's standing in her white karate uniform or *gi*, about to be attacked by another student. The martial arts instructor standing on the sidelines instructs your student to protect herself. He doesn't say: "When an opponent comes at you—use *karate*." Instead, he gives your student a specific, proven method of defense, telling her: "When your opponent comes at you, start with a left arm block, then use a fist strike."

Specific methods of self-defense are what are missing from a lot of today's cyberbullying curricula. Many websites and manuals have sharpened their resources and advice over the past decade, and there is a lot of insightful information about cyberbullying online, but there's not enough information about what to do in the face of specific tactics. What happens when a student comes to you in confidence and says, "Someone started a website about me. They stole my photo and made it look like I'm doing something I really didn't. Now I'm getting all these nasty texts and I don't know how to stop it"? Most adults would not even know where to start with this scenario. Questions that come to mind would be: What website? Who started it? How can a stolen photo be altered in such a way? Are the cell phone harassers the same ones who started the impersonating website?

Cyberbullying can take the form of dozens of tactics with each new tool. It can start on a student's cell phone or laptop, jump to social networking sites, but then manifest as traditional face-to-face bullying the next day. In other words, it's very difficult to apply general cyberbullying advice to specific situations, especially when the student, the parent, and the school authorities don't know where to start. Your student may be a target of one tactic, a combination of several, or may have contributed to the bullying himself. You won't know exactly how to fight it until you see the whole picture. This workbook will help you do just that.

We start every chapter with a hypothetical scenario based on many real-life cyberbullying incidents we pulled from the news while researching this workbook. Every scenario will have a bully and a target, but each tactic may differ in terms of whether bystanders, allies, and other parties are involved, providing a range of opportunities for students to identify with the various roles. Note: rather than use the term "victim," which many feel further stigmatizes the cyberbullying recipient, we choose to use the word "target."

To understand what motivates a bully, which kind of personality types are susceptible to being targets, and what are the psychological motives of every player who is involved in a cyberbullying incident, we strongly recommend Barbara Coloroso's smart, succinct book, *The Bully, The Bullied, and The Bystander,* as well as The Olweus Bullying Prevention Program (Teacher Guide). These two resources provide a more nuanced description of bullies, bystanders, targets, and allies. For educators, just knowing what to look for can make all the difference in proactively disengaging a potential conflict before it escalates into perpetration, harassment . . . even school violence.

Bullying vs. Cyberbullying: What's The Difference?

"Cyberbullying is the use of modern communication technologies to embarrass, humiliate, threaten, or intimidate an individual in the attempt to gain power and control over them."[10] People who don't understand how cyberbullying occurs often ask, "How can someone get *bullied* online? Can't you just turn the computer off and it's over?" The answer is "No," because the issue is not the computer, it's about the real life argument or the conflict happening between the teenagers, and that doesn't go away simply when a laptop is shut off.

As Executive Director of Net Family News, Inc., Anne Collier explains, "Digital bullying and harassment is infinitely more about our humanity than our technology, so the latter—whether it's taking a phone away, blocking aggressors on a site, or taking a profile or hate group down—isn't going to prevent or fix conflict between people, which is almost always offline as well as online."[11]

Here are other differentiations between traditional bullying and cyberbullying:

1. **It's anonymous**: With traditional bullying, the target knows who the bully is. Online, the perpetrator(s) are often hidden. "The cyberbully can cloak his or her identity behind a computer or cell phone using anonymous email addresses or pseudonymous screen names."[12]

2. **It's viral**: The power differential here relies on the sheer number of followers and bystanders a cyberbully can instantly amass. The cyberbully can spread his or her offensive messages to many more people very quickly than one used to be able to do offline. An embarrassing photo taken with a cell phone can be sent to hundreds of classmates in minutes.[13]

3. **It's not face-to-face**: Because of the anonymity of the Internet, the cyberbully doesn't see the immediate response of the target. This inability to see or hear the hurt that they are causing is called "disinhibition." It allows the cyberbully to

behave with more hostility and aggression than in typical face-to-face confrontations and prevents the cyberbully from having an empathic response to the target.[14]

4. **It's repeated aggression**: Even though it can be a one-time incident, cyberbullying is more aptly defined when "someone repeatedly makes fun of another person online or repeatedly picks on another person through email or text message or when someone posts something online about another person that they don't like."[15]

5. **It's portable**: With traditional bullying, one can leave the conflict at school and at least find respite at home for a while. With cell phones and computers, the cyberbully's messages are constantly bombarding the target wherever he or she goes.

6. **It lingers online**: Online dirt doesn't always go away. In some cases, negative and harassing messages stay archived on Internet search engines and can besmirch a target's online reputation for years unless they are removed or pushed down through adult intervention.

The point of this workbook is not to frighten or overwhelm parents and educators with a "sky-falling-down" portrayal of the Internet, but rather, to help adults fine-tune what they already know about cyberbullying dangers and use additional information in each chapter to empower the students to anticipate and navigate specific cyberbullying tactics. After reading this workbook, adults will not only be better informed about various cyberbullying tactics and how to effectively intervene, but can now be the "eyes and ears" for students who are not yet equipped to handle these situations themselves. The following section instructs educators how to use this workbook, covers the six tactics, and provides valuable advice for adults (at home and at school) on how to create a school-wide environment that is proactive and preventative before cyberbullying even starts.

How To Use This Workbook

For teachers who are continuously operating under time constraints, these chapters are set up to be used *in sections* for multiple class periods, ideally over the course of one school semester. You can pick and choose, you can skip around, or you can use certain sections as experiential learning hands-on exercises to reflect what's going on in the news and real life. The point is you don't have to use the whole workbook in chronological order of each chapter presented, and you don't have to do it all in one class period.

Age Appropriate Chapters for Younger vs. Older Teens

You'll find that some of the tactics outlined in this workbook are more sophisticated than others, and some will be more appropriate for certain age groups and genders than others. Older teens are more computer-literate than younger tweens and tend to have more social media experience and less parental restrictions. In line with published studies evaluating students ages 12–17, the risk of being bullied is higher for older adolescents and lower for younger adolescents.[16] Therefore, we targeted this workbook to an audience that ranges from middle school (5th grade) to high school (12th grade).

How To Start

1. Assess the age group of your class.
2. Review the six tactics in the next section and determine which chapter best fits the age and technological sophistication of your class.
3. Give your students the Student Survey To Assess Which Tactics to Cover in **Appendix A**. The results will help assess what technological skills and applications your students are already using and determine which tactics to cover.

The Six Cyberbullying Tactics

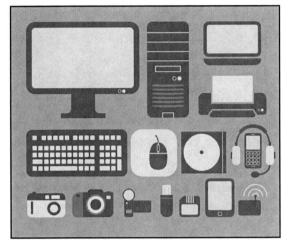

Using The Internet

1. **Digital Pile On**: This relational aggression tactic is when a group led by a ringleader bullies an individual in an online social setting, such as a chat forum. Here, the bully sees an opportunity to belittle the target while obtaining "safety in numbers." The situation escalates when bystanders provide the bully with encouragement and support.

2. **Rating Website**: With this tactic, the target either uploads a photo of himself to a rating website or a bully posts an unflattering photo of the target without his knowledge. The bully and other downraters proceed to negatively rate the target's attractiveness for the purpose of entertainment or revenge.

3. **Imposter Profile**: With this tactic, the bully creates a fake social networking profile or website to deceive others into believing it is genuinely owned and maintained by the target. The profile provides humiliating, false, and incriminating information about the target and/or secret disclosures, as if the target is willingly "confessing" to this information.

4. **Haters' Club**: With this tactic, a mob is involved in bullying the target, often prompted by discriminatory aspects like race, gender, or sexual orientation. The bullies start up a website or social networking profile with the target's image and denigrating information so that followers can persistently defame the target's reputation with name-calling, misinformation, lies, and other forms of harassment.

Using a Cell Phone

5. **Sexting:** In this tactic, the target bears the responsibility of sending a nude and/or explicitly sexualized photo of himself or herself by cell phone or digital camera to a romantic partner. When the relationship ends or turns sour, the

recipient of this photo may turn into the perpetrator by deliberately forwarding the photo electronically to other recipients or posting the photos publicly on the Internet. An innocent recipient may also become an unwitting perpetrator by forwarding the photo electronically to the authorities. In other cases, a third party may find or hijack the cell phone containing the Sexting photo, then circulate it by cell phone or upload it to a website, unbeknownst to either the sender or the recipient of the photo.

Using A Digital Camera/ Video Camera

6. **Videojacking**: This tactic refers to a bully who videotapes the target on a cell phone, digital camera, or camcorder, or else finds existing footage and uploads potentially embarrassing or denigrating video online to popular video-sharing sites like YouTube without the express permission or knowledge of the target.

The Four Steps To Cyberbullying

Understand, Prevent, Combat, and Transform

Each chapter is organized in four steps, in logical order of how cyberbullying occurs:

- **Understand** the tactics and the motivations of the bullies, bystanders, targets, and allies;
- **Prevent** the potential areas of interpersonal conflict through behavioral and technological self-defense;
- **Combat** the tactic ethically and legally; and
- **Transform** a negative experience into a self-empowering one.

1.   Understand

The Understand section of each chapter defines what the specific cyberbullying tactic is, how it's done, and what typical roles students will take around the tactic. Most of the time, students won't even know that they've gotten themselves involved in a particular tactic (or combination of) until it is too late. With this section, students will begin to develop insight into what motivates each person to participate in a cyberbullying situation. Beyond the goal of helping students avoid being targeted, an additional aim with these sections is to teach potential bullies how to recognize their own destructive behavior as well as motivate bystanders to take the risk to become the target's allies. The fictionalized story scenario at the beginning of each chapter will help students identify with the various motivations behind each role. Below is a basic primer on the four major roles to a cyberbullying incident.

Roles: As defined by the *Olweus Bullying Prevention Program*[17]

- **Bully/bullies** start the incident
- **Followers/henchmen** take an active part in the incident, but don't start the incident
- **Supporters/passive bullies** support the bullying, but don't take an active part in the incident
- **Passive supporters** agree with the bullying, but don't take any active part in supporting the incident
- **Disengaged onlookers** observe the bullying but do not take a stand on either side
- **Possible defenders** don't like the bullying but don't go so far as to actually defend the target
- **Defenders of the target** take a stand to defend the target.

2.   Prevent

The Prevent section of each chapter is the key to every student's choice to engage or not engage in cyberbullying. As we continually emphasize, cyberbullying isn't just about the technological tools, it's about the behavior. When we look a little deeper into what causes interpersonal conflict, we start to build an awareness that keeps us from blindly reacting to harm. Without conflict resolution skills, students using digital media will inevitably encounter the same behavioral issues over and over. Therefore, each Prevent section offers a conflict resolution lesson pertaining to a particular cyberbullying tactic. These conflict resolution exercises are integral to understanding and preventing misunderstandings and grievances before they end up online. Additionally, each Prevent section includes advice on how to maintain a smart defense from potential conflicts using behavioral and technological tips.

The other side to effective prevention is cultivating a moral and ethical sense in teenagers to break the code of silence in observing verbal, physical, or electronic taunts and to take a stand as an ally. Internationally recognized author of *Queen Bees and Wannabes*, Rosalind Wiseman, recounts her frustration when people imply that teens have always been mean to one another and bullying has been around forever. "The minute somebody says that," Wiseman says in a podcast interview she did with fellow educator Annie Fox, "that is *the* minute when critically thinking people stop and say, 'Why?!' Because if it involves the degradation of other people—especially if it's done for the entertainment of other people like bystanders—then that is a problem, and that is a tradition that needs to be challenged immediately."[18]

3.   Combat

In each Combat section, the workbook provides escalating hypothetical scenarios to help students recognize the difference between mild teasing and serious threats. To clarify, we use the term *combat* from a martial artist's perspective: to mentally prepare, defend, and use one's positive energy and wisdom to fight the negative energy/tactic that appears as the threat. This is not suggesting that targets should retaliate or engage in any kind of combat in the conventional sense. We make this distinction because many of the students in our workshops reported they'd confront the bully if provoked, or retaliate in kind. For a lot of kids, that's the only way they know to stop it. Yet, instructing teenagers to verbally or physically "fight back" or deal with it by themselves can be just as destructive as telling them to "just ignore it." Without self-awareness or knowledge of how to effectively resolve conflict, revenge and retaliation tend to be the default reaction and most definitely will make the outcome much worse. Statistics show that youth who engage in online aggressive behavior by making rude or nasty comments or frequently embarrassing others are more than twice as likely to report online interpersonal victimization.[19]

Being strategic about how to react is the key to combating and overcoming the tactic. Proper support from parents, effective intervention from educators, and a school-wide policy in place are the most effective ways to combat a cyberbullying situation. Students need to know that they do have civil and legal rights and that the bully isn't going to get away with it. A safe environment in which targets and bystanders can report the wrongdoing is also critical. As Anne Collier, co-director of ConnectSafely.org, expounds, "We also need to break the code of silence that adults themselves condition in kids by telling them from early childhood on that it's bad to 'tattle'."[20]

The fictionalized scenario at the beginning of each chapter will help targeted students distinguish what appropriate level of action to take. From the Homeland Security Advisory System, we've adapted an easy-to-understand Threat Level Assessment. From advice given to us by Washington school attorney Thomas Hutton and the Maine State Police Computer Crimes Unit as well as specific advice on Sexting given to us by Illinois attorney Joshua Herman, every Threat Level Assessment in this workbook has been analyzed to help educators and students identify what legal and ethical steps to take to combat the particular threat the student is facing.

In a cyberbullying situation, how do you determine what really happened? Sometimes an incident looks clear-cut, but other times it is a convoluted mess. It is difficult for administrators to know how a conflict started, if multiple perpetrators were involved, or if the target retaliated. To get all the facts, administrators need to record the incident in writing. See our **Scene Survey** Worksheet in **Appendix B** to aid in this fact-finding effort.

4.   Transform

The Transform section of each cyberbullying tactic was constructed assuming a student has already been emotionally injured. We wanted to provide a section to this workbook that no other cyberbullying curriculum has incorporated as part of the lesson plan. This was prompted by our own early experiences with this project. At the end of one of our workshops, two middle school girls came up to us and confided that they'd both been badly cyberbullied by a group of girls of a different race. "They've always hated me," one of the girls told us, her eyes fixed on the lunchroom table. "I don't understand why they hate me." After making sure she had already alerted the school administrators, we tried to explain that her bullies were just looking for anything—a weakness, a difference to go after—and that it wasn't really about her. We advised her that once her school administrators addressed the problem, the bullies would stop what they were doing and move on. Her eyes trailed away. It was obvious we'd just given the typical adult "lip service" and she didn't believe us. Thinking about it later, we felt we'd let her down. How did we know it would eventually go away? How do you help cyberbullying targets overcome feelings of worthlessness and depression after the fact? More importantly, what can we do as a community to prevent extremely bullied students from feeling they have no way out, no one to turn to?

For the purpose of helping victimized teens transform negative experiences into positive lessons for growth, we turned to Chuck Nguyen, a martial artist/bullying expert, to translate Eastern philosophies of resilience and self-defense into each chapter. For the past twenty years of teaching Kung Fu and fifteen years of clinical social work, Nguyen has found similarities in martial arts training and how someone deals with personal and social issues. From Chinese Kung Fu to the Japanese practice of Aikido, the basis of all techniques is how to transform energy or aggression into the defender's advantage and to end harm as effectively and quickly as possible. With bullying and cyberbullying, there is a range of harmful behaviors, from mild teasing to malicious intent. Each Transform section assumes the target has suffered from malicious intent. To transform the pain caused by cyberbullying, a student must be ready to counter with practiced and rehearsed methods that create minimal harm and most effective results, and to come away from a negative cyberbullying experience with a productive and positive mentality.

Beyond the martial arts angle, it's necessary to include a psychological perspective in transforming a bad experience. The Youth Voice Research Project, co-authored by Stan Davis and Charisse Nixon, PhD, is the first known large-scale research project that solicits students' perceptions about how to reduce peer mistreatment in our schools. Davis, a school counselor and child and family therapist, said that two things help mistreated kids disconnect their feelings from others' behaviors:

1. **Support from peers**: The more connections young people have, the more likely they are to be able to see negative actions toward them as the work of a few people who are acting immature (a phrase that came up in our research many times as kids talked about the way they came to understand and deal with mean behavior). These relationships *demonstrate* to the mistreated student that he or she is valued and is part of the school. Those two factors—a sense of belonging and a sense of being valued at school—connected in our study with lower rates of traumatization, as did kids going to adults for help. That sense of being valued and belonging helps kid see that the mean behavior is the fault of their tormentors, not theirs.

2. **Support from adults**: In addition, resiliency is about kids knowing that they are not helpless—that they have options including getting support. Youth reported being told not to tattle was the most damaging action adults could do in the face of mistreatment. Close behind this was being told if the 'student had acted differently,' the mistreatment wouldn't have happened. These adult actions deter youth from seeking help and thus isolate them and make them more vulnerable. This, in turn, makes it harder for youth to see that the mean behavior is the mistreater's fault.

Davis and Nixon also offered advice that students in The Youth Voice Project gave in terms of what will and won't work after a traumatic bullying incident. The students said what works or makes things better is:
- being truly listened to by someone; having the whole story come out;
- getting emotional support from their friends and their parents;
- having adults check back over time;
- having ongoing supervision;
- having peers walk with and spend time with mistreated youth.

What doesn't work or makes it worse:

- telling the bully how "they feel" and trying to change the behavior of the bully;
- physically attacking the bully;
- making plans for retaliation against the bully.[21]

To find more information on The Youth Voice Research Project, visit our Resources section online.

In many cyberbullying situations, a teenager is often overpowered the moment conflict starts online because the fighting weight is typically unbalanced. The anonymity of the Internet skews this balance. The target often finds he isn't facing one or two aggressors; he is up against potentially hundreds (and in some viral situations, thousands) of aggressors hiding behind their keyboards. This is why it's crucial for adults to be the protectors and help balance the fighting weight. The following advises parents, school staff, and school administrators how to do that.

Adults: How You Can Help

For Parents

"It's Ten O' Clock: Do You Know What Site Your Child Is On?"

Only a short number of years ago, parents had more control over the type of online media their children viewed, because home and school computers were the only way to access the Internet. Today, with the number of electronic devices teens are given and use, Internet access is 24-7. A publication "Using the Media to Promote Adolescent Well-Being" from the collaborative project, The Future of Children, recognizes the modern morass of technology parents find themselves in now that Internet accessibility is everywhere—on their children's computers, cell phones, iPods, Tablet PC, gaming consoles, etc. "The increasing portability of new media platforms means that youth can access most media outside the supervision of parents or other responsible adults. The brute fact is that even the most vigilant parents cannot supervise their teenagers at every moment."[22]

Knowing what kind of content your teenager is accessing at any hour of the day is crucial to knowing what else is shaping his or her perceptions of the world. It starts with discussions over what kind of online media your teenager is drawn to . . . and why.

How Do I Start?

Start by crafting a house policy on acceptable Internet media use for your child. See our Parent/Student contract in **Appendix E** and our Resources for more information. Some guidelines to discuss with your teenager:

- Have you discussed with your child exactly which websites, social networking profiles, and Internet or gaming communities he or she is allowed to sign up for? Do you allow your child to do so if he is under the required age? If so, do you and your child have a clear understanding about his or her responsibilities on these sites?

- Have you and your children set a house policy on where they can access the Internet, how to stick to time limits, how to use privacy settings, and how to make good choices online while behaving responsibly? Does this include: no "trash talking," cyberbullying, Sexting, or chatting with strangers?

- Do you have an agreement with them to have the passwords to their social networking sites and cell phones if their behavior gives you a reason to be concerned or you need to access their passwords for their safety's sake?

- Do you instruct them not to post anything potentially too revealing (who they like, where they can be found after school) or anything embarrassing that can be used against them? Do you impose consequences for use and misuse of their media?

My Kid Is Being Cyberbullied. Who Can Help?

Many parents express a sense of being overwhelmed, of not knowing where to start or who to go to for help when their child is targeted by cyberbullying. Though we offer many hypothetical options in the Combat section of this workbook, each individual case takes careful consideration and strategic intervention. Kids are often hesitant to tell an adult in school for fear that "snitching" will cause them to be perceived as weak and unable to stand up for themselves. They're also afraid to tell their parents for fear that a) the parents may react in a knee-jerk fashion, which worsens the situation or b) the parents will take away their tech gadget (cell phones, computer, iPod Touch) the very devices they need to monitor the ongoing cyberbullying situation if it escalates. Here are your options:

- **Get The Full Story**: Everything starts with a household investigation. Use The **Scene Survey (Appendix B)** to assess whether this is a one-on-one cyberbullying situation, a group gang-up, a mild "teasing" incident, or a more severe harassment. Understand your teen may only be able to give you one perspective and that likely there is more to the story, but start by gathering as much factual information as you can.[23]

- **Parent-To-Parent Discussion**: This can be very tricky in the way it is handled, but done calmly and thoughtfully, it can help resolve the situation. Acknowledge that you are presenting your kid's "truth" and don't make assumptions until you've heard the other "truths" to the story as well. Present yourself as a reasonable person willing to see both sides. With skillful communication, you may be able to resolve the situation yourselves, among parents (working with your kids), but anticipate that some parents will be prone to reacting negatively, regardless of your demeanor. Keep electronic proof of the bullying (*except* in the case of Sexting: refer to Chapter 5) to show parents, school authorities, and police, if necessary.[24]

- **Contact the School Officials**: Do not accept the common dismissal that if it happened "off-campus" it isn't their problem. If the cyberbullying affects your child's or other children's behavior within school and disrupts even a single child's ability to learn, it is their responsibility to address it.[25]

- **Contact the Website or Service Provider**: Filing an abuse report at the source of the cyberbullying incident is a start—but it won't get to the root of the behavior. You will also need a court document such as a subpoena to get service providers to release the identity of other users due to US privacy laws.[26]

- **Getting The Police & Lawyers Involved**: This is the highest level of your fighting weight. This option needs to be carefully considered when there is serious harassment/threats, criminal behavior, extortion, obscene or harassing phone calls/texts, stalking, hate crimes, child pornography, sexual exploitation, or when the target's photograph has been taken in a place where he or she would expect privacy and is now being misused.[27]

For Educators

As an educator, you are probably already undertaking more roles than you ever thought possible when you first started teaching. One more role in any bullying or cyberbullying situation is that of *protector*. Your status within the adult organization doesn't matter to the kids. Even support staff such as a school janitor, office staff, or a school bus driver have a legal duty to act in the best interest of the children in their care, providing a safe environment from bullies and other harm. If the parent doesn't have the capacity to be an advocate for the target, you are next in line as the student's protector. If you observe or become aware of a student being bullied or cyberbullied and you need the help of others to effectively intervene, don't hesitate to pull them in.

How Do I Start?

Start by crafting a classroom policy on acceptable Internet media use for your students. See our Parent/Student contract in **Appendix E** and our Resources for more information. Some guidelines in dealing with a classroom cyberbullying:

- Does your school have a school policy on both bullying and cyberbullying?
- Do you have classroom rules regarding respect and consideration of others?

- Do your students know that being online or using a cell phone within school is a privilege and do they practice Netiquette? What are your classroom consequences for those who disobey these rules?

- Do you encourage them to periodically change their passwords and remind them never to share them?

- Do they feel they can come to you if they are cyberbullied or harassed online? Have you made them aware of resources both in and out of school that can help them?

- Do you know the legal ramifications of being shown a Sexting photo by one of your students and the consequences of forwarding it to authorities? If not, join with other teachers to request that your administration adopt our school policy template in **Appendix D**.

For School Authorities

Many schools already have "bully/harassment" policies in place, but with the way cyberbullying is morphing and changing with each new technological fad, it's becoming necessary for schools to put a strategic plan around this issue—not just a policy, but a "whole-school response." Anne Collier, Executive Editor of NetFamilyNews.org, suggests: "School communities need to do both situational and culture-change work; situational is incident-related ("teachable moments") and culture-change or culture-of-respect work is obviously ongoing and involves all community members, including parents."[28]

How Do I Start?

To start, here are essential questions to ask of your school culture:

- Do you currently have a school policy on both bullying and cyberbullying?

- Have you trained your staff on what to do in the event of bullying/cyberbullying?

- Has your staff been trained on the legal ramifications of being shown a Sexting photo by a student and what protocols are needed in contacting the authorities?

- Do you require parent/student contracts around acceptable Internet use?

- Are you implementing a comprehensive cyberbullying prevention curriculum to educate your students about how to protect themselves from various tactics?

- Do you have sufficient reporting mechanisms in place or offer an anonymous tip line to break the code of silence in your school?

- Do the students have at least one trained school resource person they can trust to go to regarding cyberbullying incidents if their parents can't or won't be their advocate?

First: Determine What Constitutes Acceptable Behavior

The authors of *Developing Emotional Intelligence* contend that if a school doesn't have behavioral expectations of their students from the beginning, "it's unfair to expect people to behave in any manner other than how they have been taught to behave."[29]

Determine what constitutes acceptable and unacceptable behavior (both offline and online), allowing staff to have consensus on what students' rights and responsibilities should be and anything that will have a "profoundly negative impact on the school climate."[30]

Second: Train Your Staff

Maintaining a culture of respect is an ongoing need and opportunity because it lowers the risk level. In a podcast discussion with educator Annie Fox, educator and author Rosalind Wiseman advises, "Don't do a 45-minute assembly on cyberbullying. It's a waste of time." She suggests starting with a faculty meeting first to get your entire faculty (particularly guidance counselors and school psychologists) on board with your cyberbullying rules and policy. Inform the parents next at parent meetings to gain buy-in. Lastly, inform the students what their roles, responsibilities, and consequences are around harassment and cyberbullying. Says Wiseman, "Tell [the students] 'we understand that this is about the whole culture of the school, and as part of that culture, you have to participate in this as well'."[31]

Third: Provide A Safe Outlet For Reporting Or An Anonymous Tipline

The other major issue that pervades schools is the culture of silence around bullying/cyberbullying. No one wants to "snitch" and many bystanders and potential allies express discomfort in standing up to a bully for fear they'll be the next target. For schools to have an effective anti-bullying school-wide environment, every student should be encouraged, and every staff member required, to report any situation that they believe to be bullying, harassment, or aggressive behavior directed toward a student. Reports by students may also be made anonymously by calling SpeakOut Hotline at 1-800-226-7733 or going online to SchoolTipline at http://www.schooltipline.com.

Fourth: Determine Disciplinary Action . . . Individually

As for disciplinary measures, one suspension does not fit all. "A school may try to help resolve a situation informally without immediately taking disciplinary action, for example, by notifying the bully and his or her parents," says Seattle school attorney Thomas Hutton.[32]

"It's about turning an incident into a teachable moment," says Anne Collier, Executive Director of Net Family News, Inc. "The goal is to stop the victimization as quickly as possible and make as many people learn from the incident as possible so the same mistake isn't repeated. Student suspension cannot be the only response, much less a 'zero tolerance' response leading reflexively to suspension. It is like a blunt-instrument approach that of course punishes some involved—*if* they like being in school—but discourages students from reporting such cases in the future and doesn't resolve what the argument was about."[33]

Shanterra McBride, cyberbullying expert and Founder/Director of Preparing Leaders of Today, echoes the need to put individualized consequences (not just suspension) in place. Among her recommendations is to require the bully to publicly apologize using the same digital tool he or she cyberbullied with, as well as apologize to the school community for violating the respectful culture that the school worked to create.[34]

Steps for Effective Intervention

We encourage adults to approach a cyberbullying incident in exactly the same way we instruct students in this workbook:

- **Cool Off**: Take time to cool off and talk it through before making an emotional snap judgment about the bully's actions. The emotional mind works much faster than the rational mind and skips important steps when you are angry and upset. Don't react when you are in "flight or fight mode" out of defensiveness and anger and wait until your rational mind has had a chance to catch up.
- **Perspective Gathering**: To get to the bottom of the issue, gather additional perspective from as many other students and adults who were directly involved using our **Scene Survey (Appendix B)** (be careful in the case of Sexting—see Chapter 5). Remember: what may at first appear to be clear-cut may, in fact, only be a snapshot in an ongoing, more complicated conflict.
- **Make A Plan**: Consult our Threat Level Assessment in the "Combat" section of each chapter. It will help you gauge how mild or how serious the incident really is in order to proceed with a plan.

Where Cyberbullying Happens

Depending on where cyberbullying happens, off-campus or on, whose responsibility it is to address it? The parents or the school administrators?

Whether and how a school may intervene with individual cyberbullying incidents depends on several factors, according to Seattle school attorney, Thomas Hutton. "If the bullying is occurring on campus or is clearly having a negative impact on campus, the school district's cyberbullying policy, if any, will indicate what action may be taken. The authority of public schools over private online expression, even bullying, is limited," Hutton emphasizes. "If the school district has a cyberbullying policy, the policy should reflect these cautions."[35]

What if the incident happened at home? Hutton advises: "The school's response may vary depending on its policies, if any, about cyberbullying, and important legal constraints, especially where the bullying may have occurred entirely off-campus, and as yet has had no clear impact on campus. Even where the school's disciplinary authority may be limited, however, bullying behavior may violate the legal rights of victims in ways that can be pursued directly by the victim or by law enforcement."[36]

Nancy Willard, MS, JD, author of *Cyberbullying Legislation and School Policies*, also weighs in on what happens when cyberbullying at home crosses the school line:

> We have to start with this question: If the off-campus speech of a student or students is such that it has, or there are good reasons to believe it could, lead to violent altercations between students at school, create an environment that makes it impossible for a student to feel safe coming to school or to effectively participate in learning, or cause an overall significant disruption in the delivery of instruction to many students, would any reasonable person argue that school officials should not have the authority to respond with formal discipline?

> Fortunately, the case law in this area clearly establishes that school officials have the authority to respond to student off-campus speech if that speech has or could cause a substantial disruption at school. A leading decision on bullying prevention policies noted that speech that has caused a significant interference in the ability of any student to receive an education is almost by definition a substantial disruption.

However, it is important for districts to specifically address this in their policies, so that students have notice. The trend in state statutes and district policies is to specifically indicate that schools have the authority to respond to off-campus student speech that has or could cause a substantial disruption at school or interference with the ability of any student to be secure and receive an education.[37]

School Policy and Parent/Student Contract Templates

Along with the advice in each chapter, we provide administrative templates for a school-wide cyberbullying prevention policy to encourage the adoption of such procedures in school districts throughout the country.

- **SCHOOL POLICY**

  For schools everywhere, we developed a comprehensive school policy in **Appendix D** based on research from cyberbullying experts, governing agencies, and school administrator input. This policy constitutes what is acceptable and unacceptable behavior in school, specifically defines what constitutes cyberbullying, and provides a range of solutions for lighter cases and consequences for more serious cases, while representing an appropriate balance between student free speech rights and the safety and security of students at school. Use this replicable template to enact or expand upon your current school policy to broaden the definition of traditional bullying and harassment. This policy can also be copied and pasted from our online Resources.

- **PARENT/STUDENT CONTRACTS**

  When the rules and consequences for cyberbullying are stated up front and consistently applied, students have the choice to "own" their behavior. Our sample "Acceptable Use for Technology" contract requires that each parent reads and explains the rules to his or her child. For some parents who are unable or unwilling to read and sign this contract, make it conditional that a student does not have access to an unsupervised, non-portable computer on school time without signing the contract. See **Appendix E**. This contract can also be copied and pasted from our online Resources.

one

Internet Tactics: Digital Pile On

Digital Pile On:

When everyone jumps on top of one unfortunate soul, they "pile on."

—Urban Dictionary

This relational aggression tactic is when a group, led by a ringleader, bullies an individual in an online social setting such as a chat forum. Here, the bully sees an opportunity to belittle the target while obtaining "safety in numbers." The situation escalates when bystanders provide the bully with encouragement and support.

Getting Started

Lesson Rundown Students are introduced to the concept of a common tactic called a Digital Pile On, which uses group intimidation to single out an individual in a digital environment.

Objective: Students will be able to:

- understand relational aggression tactics better in an online setting;
- make deliberate choices to communicate positively or negatively online;
- assess how to defend themselves ethically and legally in escalating situations;
- practice mental calmness in the aftermath of a Digital Pile On.

Time Needed The Understand, Combat, and Transform sections are structured to be conducted within a typical classroom requiring 30-40 minutes of lesson time. The Prevent sections may require 30-60 minutes as they go more in-depth and may prompt more conversation. Total estimated time for the Digital Pile On Unit is 2-3 hours, and will vary in an after-school or workshop environment.

Teacher Prep Read chapter ahead of class time and refer to the sections labeled "For The Educator." Review any group or individual activities ahead of time for materials needed to maximize in-class time.

Equipment/ Supplies Needed Computers with Internet access can be used for activities labeled with high-tech. Otherwise, paper and writing materials can be used for those labeled low-tech.

Vocab Words Defined at the end of this section

Handouts *Reframing Exercise, Chat Acronym List, Threat Level Assessments*

For The Educator

> ## Tactic Overview
>
> This chapter focuses on how a Digital Pile On starts, who participates, and ways to help students proactively avoid falling victim to this type of tactic. It also deals with the most basic elements of conflict and behavior. Students will learn how to protect themselves when they are socializing online and what to do if they have been a target of a Digital Pile On.

How A Digital Pile On Happens: The Internet has its own culture and rules, something young people don't always grasp as they navigate through this territory. A Digital Pile On reflects adolescent behavior that has always been around, whether it is offline or online. Students assume they are only communicating with their friends when, in fact, their messages are broadcast to a vast invisible audience. These are classic communication mistakes made by **newbies**. Compounding the problem is the fact that unsupervised online areas often breed incivility. A 2009 AP-MTV Digital Abuse Study found that nearly half of young people (45%) report that they see people being mean to each other on social networking sites.[38]

With a Digital Pile On, there is almost always a ringleader, someone with a grudge or a motivation. Dr. Rick Brinkman and Dr. Rick Kirchner, authors of *Dealing With People You Can't Stand: How to Bring Out the Best in People at Their Worst,* have a term for this type of ringleader: a **Sniper**. With the anonymity and protection of closed Internet communities, and armed with a motive, the Sniper has the perfect opportunity to attack with rude comments, sarcastic humor, and biting commentary, much to the amusement of the **followers**. Since "the Sniper's limited power is derived from covert, not overt, activity," say the authors, the key to dealing with a Sniper is "forcing her out of her hiding place and onto common ground."[39] For more on how to disable the Sniper, see the Combat section.

Most teachers will recognize the "ganging up" aspect in our opening scenario. It's a familiar behavioral tactic of girls, which reflects current studies that demonstrate girls are noticeably more likely to engage in cyberbullying than boys.[40] Still, other experts caution against painting the online behavior of girls with the same brush. "There's a tendency to hype up and overplay the mean girl phenomenon," says Rachel Simmons, author of *Odd Girl Out: The Hidden Culture of Aggression in Girls*. She contends that girls eventually outgrow some of the behavior.[41] Lyn Mikel Brown, EdD, author of *Girlfighting: Betrayal and Rejection Among Girls,* explores the deeper undertones to girls' online behavior. "We are all complex beings with the capacity to do harm and to do good, sometimes within the same hour," she says. "Talk to your class about specific behaviors, why they're hurtful, and how best to understand them and respond. Labels such as 'bullies' or 'mean girls' are fixed; behavior can change."[42]

In a Digital Pile On, the power of one bully lies in numbers; the bully isn't successful unless there is an audience. When technology instantaneously allows a bully to reel in his or her followers, this tactic becomes more powerful and particularly hurtful when multiple **bystanders** lend the perception that they're all teaming up to "get" the target, particularly when the behavioral tactics of **flaming**, **trolling**, **name-calling**, **group self-congratulation**, and **exclusion** are employed.

Note: we've chosen to display this tactic using the Group Chat function on Google Talk, (similar to the Gmail chat box but with multiple people) but it can also be done on any Instant Relay Connection (IRC) application, including Twitter, virtual worlds, and social networking "Walls" that allow multiple users to see each other's instant comments.

VOCAB WORDS

Bystander: A person who is present at an event without participating in it.

Exclusion: Intentionally rejecting someone from an online group, such as on a "buddy list," Facebook group, or game.

Flaming: Online "fights" using electronic messages with angry and/or vulgar language.

Followers: People who don't start the bullying, but join in and have the potential to escalate it.

Name-Calling: Verbal abuse, especially as a crude form of argument.

Newbie: One that is new to something, especially a novice at using computer technology or the Internet.

Group Self-Congratulation: Acknowledgment of a group's superiority or good fortune.

Sniper: One who attacks other people from a concealed place, defined by the authors of *Dealing With People You Can't Stand.*

Trolling: Intentionally posting provocative messages about sensitive subjects to create conflict, upset people, and bait them into "flaming" or fighting.

Scenario
Alyssa's Story

For more interactivity, print the below story and hand out to the students in order for them to act out the parts of each character and narrator.

A Bad Convo on Google Talk

Of all the dumbest things, it had started one day after school on Google Talk, when Alyssa, 11, was chatting with her friends about who was the shortest person in their class. Four other girls logged on who were on Alyssa's buddy list, including Janita, the tallest girl in their class.

Alyssa: im the shortest!

Alyssa: Janita, Ur like an Amazon.

[Then the weirdest thing happened. All of a sudden Alyssa saw:]

Janita: Alyssa-ur mean!!

Kaitlynn: ya Alyssa-wat ur prob?

Xiomy: why don't u shut up Alyssa

Beba: ur ugly and u cant grow out of that!

Janita: LOL! Beba U crack me up

Alyssa: No! I was just saying J's the tallest in our class that's all!

Janita: We don't listen to no short peeps. If ur short, u have nuttin to say.

Xiomy: that's why no guys like you*high five***

Beba: no girls either *wut up*

Alyssa: stop doing this!!!

Xiomy: no

Kaitlynn: don't tell us wat 2 do

Alyssa: now U are ALL being mean! Wasn't trying 2 hurt her feelins

Janita: wahh

Beba: u gonna tell?

Xiomy: if u gonna tell we don't want u here

Alyssa: im not gonna tell but stop!

Kaitlynn: Im not talking 2 u

Beba: me neither

Janita: bye shorty—and I don't mean that in a good way!

Xiomy: snap

Alyssa: why cant u leave me alone!!

Janita: I don't hear any1, do u?

Kaitlynn: Nope

Xiomy: crickets

Janita: lets pretend shes not here

Step I: Understand

Objective:	Students will be able to:

- identify with the roles of a bully, follower, or a defender;
- understand specific negative behaviors associated with this tactic;
- make deliberate choices to communicate positively online.

Time Needed	35 minutes.
Teacher Prep	Read any passage ahead of class time labeled "For the Educator."
Equipment/ Supplies Needed	Copier. Computers with Internet access (high-tech) or paper and pencils (low-tech).
Vocab Words	Defined at the end of this section.

Overview

Start with Topic for Discussion and then gradually move on to show your students the various roles people play in this particular tactic.

Establish Group Guidelines	See the guidelines in **Appendix C** in order to get the most out of your group discussions in class.
Topic For Discussion	With the five girls in this Scenario, ask your students to identify who is the target and who is the bully. Then ask who are the followers. Write what they say on the blackboard.
Define Tactic	Define what a Digital Pile On is to your students. Ask them if they've ever been on the ganging-up side of a Digital Pile On without realizing what it is.
For The Student: A Broader Perspective	Online conflict isn't always clear-cut. Once you've gotten through the Topic For Discussion, summarize for your students the actual roles of each participant as outlined below.

From The Bully's Perspective: Janita, an 11-year-old girl, is insecure about her height. She hates being so tall compared to all the rest of the girls in her class, and when Alyssa jokingly tried to compare her to an Amazon, Janita failed to see the humor. Instead, she took it as a direct insult and became offended. When she wrote back, "Ur mean!" she was relieved to see her friends take her side and not Alyssa's. Feeling more supported in her anger, Janita felt safe to release her insecurities by targeting Alyssa; in effect, showing Alyssa how it felt to be targeted.

From The Target's Perspective: When Alyssa left the Group Chat, she felt so bad she wanted to cry. The first thing she did was blame herself. "What did I say that made them so mad?" she questioned herself. What she thought was an innocent, even funny comment, wasn't interpreted the same way online.

It is very common to "misread" something someone says online because often conversations are quick, offered without much forethought and the written word is not accompanied by tone, inflection, or facial gestures. For this reason, online communication often leads to a misunderstanding, which is a typical source of conflict. Alyssa could see the misunderstanding grow into something more hurtful. The more the conversation went out of control, the more powerless she felt. All of a sudden, the other girls switched tactics very fast— instead of the real issue (the joke about Janita's height) they started hitting back at Alyssa with other jabs about her looks and her "status" within their group—all very sophisticated tactics from girls who didn't even understand what they were doing. At the same time, Alyssa's own behavior added fuel to the fire. Feeling cornered, she tried to defend herself and struck back by calling the rest of the girls "mean," which now gave the whole group a reason to pretend to be offended. A better strategy to stop the conflict would have been to log off and apologize to Janita alone and in person for the original misunderstanding. The best thing a target can do in this scenario is to clearly state he or she isn't trying to start conflict but won't tolerate any more abusive behavior either—then get off the Group Chat.

From The Followers' Perspective: The other girls probably wouldn't have even thought about the Amazon comment if Janita hadn't made a big deal about it. But as soon as they saw Janita was offended, they rallied around her and ganged up against Alyssa. The more Alyssa's tone came off as increasingly desperate and upset, the more the other girls jumped on her. Thinking they were defending Janita, they were actually bonding, enjoying the feeling of control and power. The conversation began instantly to veer into **flaming** and name-calling when Xiomy said, "why don't u shut up Alyssa" and Beba said, "ur ugly and u cant grow out of that!"

Encouraged by one another's boldness, the girls then continued to layer in a new behavioral tactic called **trolling**, with Janita writing: "We don't listen to no short peeps. If ur short, u have nuttin to say" and Xiomy adding, "that's why no guys like you *high five*" Finally, the girls did what they knew would be most hurtful. They used **exclusion** to make Alyssa feel insignificant and isolated.

Group Activity   Go over the vocabulary words at the end of this section as well as the last section. Then assemble small groups of three-to-four students and ask each group to identify (on the blackboard or on a piece of paper) which of the sentences in the beginning Scenario are examples of those specific definitions.

Teacher
Takeaway Tip   As you will see from this chapter, 90% of this Digital Pile On tactic is behavioral and 10% is the use of technology, so it's important for students to begin understanding the language and behavioral "rules" when socializing online—also known as **Netiquette**.

VOCAB WORDS

Exclusion: Intentionally rejecting someone from an online group, such as on a "buddy list," Facebook group, or game.

Flaming: Online "fights" using electronic messages with angry and/or vulgar language.

Netiquette: (Net etiquette) Rules for communicating with others on the Internet.

Trolling: Intentionally posting provocative messages about sensitive subjects to create conflict, upset people, and bait them into "flaming" or fighting.

Step II: Prevent

Objective   Students will be able to:

- understand what their hidden needs are and how they behave to meet them;
- sharpen their communication skills with conflict resolution skills;
- identify good online social skills through Netiquette;
- protect themselves with behavioral and technological strategies to prevent being the target of a Digital Pile On.

Time Needed   30-60 minutes, depending on computer time (if available).

Teacher Prep   Read any passage ahead of class time labeled "For the Educator." Copy the Internet chat slang list at the end of this section for each small group.

Equipment/   A computer lab and printer would be beneficial for this section, but
Supplies Needed   the individual and group activity can both be done in low-tech clas rooms with paper and highlighter pens.

Vocab Words   Defined at the end of this section.

For The Educator: Conflict Resolution Concepts

Every one of us is motivated intrinsically by four basic psychological needs according to author William Glasser. These are:

- the need to belong;
- the need for power;
- the need for freedom;
- the need for fun.

Glasser asserts that we are continuously trying to satisfy these basic needs and when any one of these needs conflicts with one another within ourselves, "our behavior is what we choose to do to resolve the conflict."[43]   However, as Richard J. Bodine and Donna K. Crawford, authors of *Developing Emotional Intelligence,* state, when the needs of two people are clashing, "conflict resolution is next to impossible as long as one side believes its psychological needs are being threatened by another."[44]

As they are emotionally developing, most teenagers don't possess the skills yet to identify and assess their own needs when they become thwarted. Studies in adolescent brain science indicate that the frontal lobes of teenagers' brains (responsible for judgment and decision-making) don't fully develop until their early 20s.[45] Because their ability to think rationally and to act with prudence is still in progress, the development of their social skills needs much practice. This is why learning self-awareness is the key to meeting and negotiating these psychological needs. To prevent unnecessary interpersonal conflict, a student needs to identify his own behaviors and learn to skillfully read social clues. In this tactic, we're going to focus on the conflict resolution concepts of "**I Messages**" and **Reframing** by authors Kathryn Girard and Susan J. Koch from their educator manual, *Conflict Resolution in the Schools.*

Communication between two people, even face-to-face, isn't always clear or mutually under-stood, and people often don't carefully choose their words. The norm in online communica-tion is to come to the point in the fewest words possible—sometimes being so blunt that the message comes across as offensive or dismissive. One simple technique you can teach your students is called the "I Message," which allows the speaker to communicate his or her needs in an assertive but non-threatening way to the listener. Sentences that start with "You" usually put the listener on the defense (which shuts down effective communication). An "I Message" has three parts, which convey the facts about a situation as well as the speaker's emotional state.

They are:

- I feel _____(fill in the blank about your current emotion)
- when _____(something happens, somebody does something)
- because _____(underlying reason).[46]

For example: "*I feel* like you are disrespecting me *when* you take my iPod without asking, *because* I like to know where my stuff is."

Reframing is when the speaker rephrases what he wants to say so that it removes the highly emotional charged tone and language and makes the message more neutral and easier for the listener to hear and absorb. Statements should focus on the behavior or problem, not the person. In addition, if the speaker wants to be heard, he should not make threats and should leave all possibilities open. For example, instead of the speaker stating, "You always take my iPod," or, "You better not take my stuff again," he can take a breath and calmly say instead, "I wish you would ask me if it is okay to borrow my iPod."[47]

Individual Activity Provide the class with copies of the "Prevent: Individual Activity" handout at the end of this chapter. Allow them a few minutes to try and reframe each statement to make the message less threatening and more positive and clear. Ask students to share what they've written.

Self-Defense On the board, write down two columns: **Behavior** and **Tech Defense**. Ask your class to volunteer their own suggestions to prevent being the target of a Digital Pile On and follow up by presenting the strategies below.

Behavior

- **Netiquette**: Know the rules of Internet etiquette (Netiquette), i.e. how to behave in an online environment. A list of Netiquette rules can be found in our Resources online.
- **Communicate Clearly**: Avoid **sarcasm, mockery,** and sharp joking online with people you don't know well. Make sure you are careful to say what you really mean. Without being able to see and hear tone, gesture, and eye contact, words communicated online often become misinterpreted, resulting in **miscommunication**.

- **Work On Confidence**: Work on having a confident personality. Stick up for yourself, but don't be too aggressive. Make it known in a calm, confident way that you're not somebody who will put up with bullying or being picked on. Public online spaces (message boards, chat rooms) are no place to discuss your insecurities. Don't ever put yourself down online—there are too many **trolls** willing to seize on this.

- **Keep Your Defense Offline**: In a Digital Pile On, you are immediately outnumbered, so get offline. The common tendency is to want to "put out a statement" or argue your case in the same online setting in which you were attacked, but experts who've seen this happen to others say this is exactly what trolls want. They want to provoke you into getting angry and upset for their own entertainment. If you react online, you are only setting yourself up for further ridicule. If you must discuss the conflict with the bully, first get adult support to help you strategize the outcome, and do it face-to-face, not online.

- **Surround Yourself**: In a Digital Pile On, the bullies' power rests in the number of followers that back them up. So don't remain alone. Bullies pick on people they think don't have anyone to defend them. Surround yourself with good, close friends and work on those friendships by being a genuine, good friend yourself. Just tell your friends not to engage in the conflict on your behalf because it will make it worse for you.

Tech Defense

Either list the following on the blackboard, or if you have access to a computer lab (and additional time), some of these exercises can be easily done in a class period. These suggestions and practice sessions will help students learn to recognize negative tactics and positive affirmations, while encouraging them to take an active role as allies. Depending on your school's policy, have each student set up a free Google Talk gadget on his or her desktop (http://www.google.com/talk/labsedition), which will walk you through the simple steps to get a Group Chat going.

- **Create Positive Screen Names**: Negative or provocative screen names (i.e. Sxxygurl, YankeesSux) lead others to think negatively of the person behind the screen name. There is no need to create conflict where there is none. Also, for identity protection, never use your real name in a screen name.

- **Create Positive Or Neutral "I'm Away" Messages**: While it may seem funny to create snippy or negative status messages (ex: I'm bored, you're boring, so don't leave a message) the same rule above applies.
- **Trust, But Verify**: Each Google Talk **alias** on your **Friends List** may or may not be who you think it is. Each user has to sign in using his or her real username but can change the alias (the "display" name) at any time. So before you tell some big, juicy secrets to your best friend, test to make sure he or she is really that person. For example, come up with a secret question and answer that only you both know.
- **Block Users**: If you need to block a Google Talk user, follow these steps:
  1. Right-click on the person's name, and select "Remove Name;"
  2. Check the box next to "Block this person" in the dialogue box that appears, and click "OK." Blocking someone will prevent him or her from talking to you, and vice versa. Blocked users can't see when you're signed in to Google Talk, and you won't see their status in your Friends list, either.[48] Remember that misusing these features can also lead to bullying if you do this intentionally to isolate a peer or classmate and/or ask others to do the same.
- **Save Chat History**: In Google Talk you can find your saved chat history in the Chats section of Gmail. You may need it to study the tactics used and be ready for them next time and/or to preserve evidence.

Group Activity   Arrange students in small groups of 5-6. Make copies of the Chat Abbreviations in the "Prevent: Group Activity" handout at the end of this chapter.[49] Ask each group to pick three positive and three negative chat abbreviations in this list. When the group is done, ask each member to identify the conflict in the negative messages. Then ask the group to try to reframe each negative statement into something more neutral or positive using an "I Message." Ask each group to discuss with the rest of the class which negative statements they chose and which positive reframed messages they came up with.

VOCAB WORDS

Alias: The name that an individual chooses to display on his or her Friend List that may or may not be his or her real name.

Friends List: A window on Google Talk that shows all your buddies and other online contacts.

"I Message": A three-part sentence that conveys the facts as well as the speaker's emotional state.

Miscommunication: Failure to communicate clearly.

Mockery: An object of scorn or ridicule.

Reframing: Rephrasing a message to make it more neutral and easier for the listener to hear and absorb.

Sarcasm: A cutting, often ironic remark intended to wound.

Trolls: Internet slang for someone who posts negative messages in an online community to provoke other users to react.

Step III: Combat

Objective

Students will be able to:
- identify low- to high-risk online situations;
- assess possible solutions to remedy conflict without resorting to revenge;
- practice making thoughtful, deliberate choices on how to react to the threat.

Time Needed

30 minutes.

Teacher Prep

Read any section ahead of class time labeled "For the Educator." Make a copy each of the Threat Level Assessments to hand out to four small groups.

Equipment/ Supplies Needed

Copier for handouts and pencils for students.

Vocab Words

Defined at the end of this section.

In the following section we use our own version of the US Department of Defense's concept of "Threat Levels" when providing students action steps to take.

Note: the advice in this section does not purport to be legal advice. We have consulted with cyberbullying experts to help parents and students know what to do in a Digital Pile On situation.

Immediate Steps To Take
Don't Want Another Attack? Don't Fire Back

Most Digital Pile Ons like the scenario at the beginning of this chapter are at the lowest end of the cyberbullying spectrum. At the first sign of the Digital Pile On, the simplest way to nip it in the bud is to remain calm, don't let the bullies think they bothered you (even if they have) and to resist firing back with the first emotional reaction you have. If the Digital Pile On is just some teasing, not intentional harassment, it is best not to overreact. Say calmly, "When you want to talk to me with respect, you know where to find me, but I'm not going to stay here." Then leave the Group Chat. While the target can't control what the bullies will say once she leaves, she can send a clear message that she will not tolerate their behavior. As mentioned in *Dealing With People You Can't Stand*, the target's only chance to disable a Sniper's attack is to force the bully out of her position of power and onto common ground by dealing with her face-to-face.[50]

Save Chat History

With Google Talk being a downloadable gadget, not an online service provider, there is no way to Report Abuse. If real hurtful/harassing statements have been made, the target has the choice to find the text of the chat history (located in the user's Gmail account under the "Chats" label) and use the evidence to show a parent or the school administration.

Threat Level Assessment

In this section, the group activity comes before the lesson. This allows students to "pre-play" how they might react to each escalating situation. *Educators will need to make copies of the four Threat Level Assessments at the end of this chapter before the group activity can begin.*

Group Activity   Split the class into four small groups and ask them to retreat to each corner of the room. Assign each group a hypothetical situation ranging from Low-Risk to High-Risk (handouts found at the end of this chapter). Appoint a group leader to read the Threat Level Assessment on each handout and give each group a chance to write down their solutions to each hypothetical situation. After each group is done, ask the group leader (starting with Low-Risk) to read the group's suggestions out loud to the class. Educators can provide the correct answer from the "What To Do" guide below for each Threat Level.

1. **Low-Risk**: You're on a Group Chat when someone says something mildly negative or makes you feel left out. For example: "I'm not talking to u, I'm talking to her," or "I don't care, that's stupid."

   Frequency: It happens once.

   What To Do: Even if you feel you've been treated rudely, get offline immediately and do not react. That's what **trolls** want—to see you react with anger. Making a big deal of it often makes the situation much worse. Decide whether to remain on this chat conversation or not by what follows next. If it is that important to you, talk to the person face-to-face afterward and use an "I Message" like, "When we were online, I felt like you weren't respecting me . . ."

2. **Guarded Risk**: You're on a Group Chat with several people and someone starts saying rude or mean things to you. Everybody joins in using **flaming, harassment, or exclusion**. The language is more sharp and cruel, appears as an attack, uses profanity, and/or violates the terms of your school's online rules.

   Frequency: It happens even just once in the online conversation.

   What To Do: Again, to have more control and power within this conflict, it is necessary to remain calm, not overreact, and get offline so you can plan your next move. If certain people are going to treat you with this kind of disrespect, you can't reason with them on a chat box, so leave the conversation immediately. Decide if you even want these people on your Friends List—or even as friends—and report or block them if you don't. They can no longer contact you and you won't be able to see their screen names when you get back on Group Chat. Save the chat history and show a trusted adult—but consider very seriously if you want an adult at home or school to do anything, because this could start a bigger conflict with the group of people, which could be more trouble than it's worth than just to ignore them and find new friends. However, if the chat incident happened on school property, administrators may be able to look at the history transcripts of each conversation and determine if it is against policy using school equipment.

3. **Elevated Risk**: The chat conversation turns into a Digital Pile On with multiple people joining as a gang of bullies. The language becomes abusive, and people are using profanity or posting your personal information (email address, phone number) to encourage more abuse from followers on the buddy list.

   Frequency: It happens even just once in the online conversation.

   What To Do: Immediately leave the Group Chat and print out the chat history or email it to a trusted adult. The more serious the abuse and its impact on you and others, the more justified you, your parents, and/or the school administrators are in addressing the issue with the bullies and their parents. Remove all the people who participated in the Digital Pile On from your Friends List. If the conflict is ongoing, ask a friend to remain on the bully's Friend List (but don't participate). The purpose is to save anything written about you for your parents or the administrators so they can take care of it.

4. **High-Risk**: The bullies are posting lewd and/or severely **derogatory** statements about you or threatening you and encouraging others to do the same. Or someone posts "**hate speech**" (any words that disrespect your race, gender, disability, sexual orientation) or makes statements to provoke other unknown people to stalk and harass you; or—post threatening comments saying things like you will be hurt or killed.

   Frequency: It has already happened and shows no sign of stopping.

   What To Do: Save the chat transcripts and show a trusted adult immediately. Your parents should take transcripts of the chat conversation and contact your school administrators and the police. This kind of language and cyber harassment may not be protected by freedom of speech, and the police can determine if the bully is breaking the law. Hate speech or threats that are made to a student are also violations of the law. Do not deal with the bullies directly. Let the police contact the bullies' parents.

Topic For Discussion Now that everyone has had a chance to work through a mock Digital Pile On, ask your students what they are going to do the next time someone says something rude online.

VOCAB WORDS

Derogatory: Showing a critical or disrespectful attitude.

Exclusion: Intentionally rejecting someone from an online group, such as on a "buddy list," Facebook group, or game.

Flaming: Online "fights" using electronic messages with angry and/or vulgar language.

Freedom of Speech: Speech protected by the First Amendment: the freedom to speak without censorship and/or limitation.

Hate Speech: Speech not protected by the First Amendment, because it is intended to foster hatred against individuals or groups based on race, religion, gender, sexual preference, place of national origin, or other improper classification.

Trolls: Someone who intentionally posts provocative messages to create conflict, upset people, and bait them into "flaming" or fighting.

Step IV: Transform

Objective   Students will be able to:
- empathize with those who have been attacked by putting themselves in the target's shoes;
- practice making thoughtful, deliberate choices on how to react after the threat;
- "pre-play" how they would deal with another example of a Digital Pile On if it happened to them.

Time Needed   30 minutes.

Teacher Prep   Allow students to read this section by themselves. For younger students, translate the concepts for better understanding.

Equipment/   Paper and pencils for students to take notes during Topic for
Supplies Needed   Discussion.

Vocab Words   Defined at the end of this section.

Note: The Transform section is meant for the students to read on their own, as this is our advice to them directly. Present this as an in-class reading or a take-home reading assignment, and then come back as a class and introduce the Topic For Discussion. For younger students, educators might want to translate some of these concepts.

For The Student: The Damage Is Done, How To Cope

Martial artist and bullying counselor Chuck Nguyen knows what it is like to be attacked. Born in Vietnam, he came to the United States as a young boy and experienced bullying the first day he walked into his new school. He grew up learning multiple skills to deal with bullies, both behaviorally and through martial arts. One of his "tests" for his black belt students is to put the target between two fellow martial artists and allow the target to try to put up a defense for one whole minute.

Similarly, in a Digital Pile On, when you are attacked, you have to believe you are capable of standing up against the bullies, regardless of the odds against you. Remember, "standing up" doesn't always mean fighting. In this case, standing up for yourself means believing in your own **dignity** and refusing to allow yourself to become their target online again. You have to mentally compose and calm yourself rather than being reactive, which can often cause more damage. This is exactly why you don't get mad and react through the keyboard. To strengthen your self-defense in these situations, you must work on being very calm and develop a strategy.

One of the biggest fears students who've been attacked on a Group Chat have is that they will be attacked again the next time they log back on. To transform this fear, you must "**pre-play**" a future scenario and think through your possible actions or choices before it happens again. Some of the following advice may sound similar to the "Combat" section, but in actuality, it is mental practice or mental **Aikido**—clearing your mind and thinking ahead about your choices before engaging in future conflict.

The physical and spiritual practice of traditional Aikido is built upon the premise that the universe is made of energy and this energy is actually in all of our thoughts, emotions, and all of our movements. When we are attacked physically or emotionally, the bully uses his or her energy to try to lessen or destroy ours. But if we are skillful, we can gather our energy to fight back and outmaneuver the bully. It sounds strange, but if you have been hurt by an experience such as this, it has actually given you better skills and more awareness to defend yourself.

Take Stock Of The Situation Calmly

One of the important steps in defending ourselves from physical or verbal harm is to see if the harm is real or if we are misinterpreting it. We do not want to be passive, but at the same time, being too aggressive (like firing back without thinking on Group Chat) will bring you down to the bullies' level and make the situation worse for you. When you sense another attack happening online, start by asking yourself, "How do I feel right now? Should I stay online or get off?" Wait a few minutes to see if the person chatting even realizes that he or she hurt you. If you are feeling panicked or overwhelmed, you might not read the situation right and defend yourself unnecessarily, triggering more of an attack. Our emotional mind works faster than our logical mind. Give your emotions a chance to catch up to your brain and get off the Group Chat so you can plan what to do next.

It's natural at this point to want to fight back. Or you might actually feel like you are about to shut down or freeze. But to "transform" what has already happened you must believe you can defend herself against the bully and her followers as if defending against only one person.

Plan Your Next Move

To ease your anxieties: don't face a Digital Pile On alone and don't keep what happened to yourself. The bully's power comes from having supporters, so you need to gather your support system too. If you've been calm and are reading the situation correctly, then thoughtfully plan your next move. Each conflict is different so now you must ask yourself, "What is the immediate threat?" Physically put yourself in a safe place (with a friend, in a trusted teacher's office) so you can think about what was done to you and make a plan. Gather additional perspective from your friends, your parents, and a trusted adult for advice on the best way to deal with the conflict, which might be as simple as staying offline for a few days to cool off or as complex as having a mediator help you work through the interpersonal conflict with the ringleader, or having a school administrator intervene with the bully and her parents on your behalf. Whatever your next move is, do it offline, face-to-face, and do not attack the bully or her followers in either a physical or verbal way. With most mild forms of a Digital Pile On, it's best to choose your friends wisely and don't allow the bully or her followers access to your Friends List. Surround yourself with people who will respect and support you and start a new Friends List with them.

Lastly, take it from others who have been bullied very badly: *this is not about you.* Bullies use technology in twisted ways in order to feel more powerful than they are in real life. It's natural to get shaken by something like this, but you must believe whatever mistakes you may have made, you did nothing to deserve this kind of treatment. Kind people with good hearts don't abuse others—it doesn't even cross their minds. Behave better than those who treat you with such malice and hold yourself to a higher standard

Topic for Discussion Note: Students can either break off as a group (boys and girls) to discuss this and share their observations with the rest of the class, or else you can treat this as an open class discussion.

Girls A group of girls are on ganging up on you and calling you nasty names on Group Chat. What should you do first? Who else should you get help from? What is your strategy for overcoming what they've just said?

Guys A group of guys are on ganging up on you and saying lies about you on Group Chat. It's making you angry to think others might believe what they are saying. What should you do first? Who else should you get help from? What is your strategy for overcoming what they've just said?

VOCAB WORDS

Aikido: A Japanese art of self-defense that employs holds and locks and that uses the principles of nonresistance in order to debilitate the strength of the opponent.

Dignity: Being worthy of honor.

Pre-Play: In "role-playing" this means acting out the possible outcomes of the game (or scenario) before it happens.

Digital Pile On Handouts
Prevent: Individual Activity

Ask students to try to reframe the following statements so that they get the message across to the listener without starting conflict.

- Don't touch my stuff!
- I didn't ask for your opinion, did I?
- Why don't you shut up and listen to me!
- You're sitting too close to me—get away.

_____

_____

_____

_____

_____

_____

_____

_____

_____

_____

_____

_____

_____

_____

_____

_____

Prevent: Group Activity
Chat Abbreviations

AAF as a friend	**BAK** back at the keyboard
AAK alive and kicking	**BBBG** bye bye be good
AAMOF as a matter of fact	**BBIAB** be back in a bit
AAR at any rate	**BBIAF** be back in a few
AAS alive and smiling	**BBIAS** be back in a sec
AATK always at the keyboard	**BBL** be back later
ABT2 about to	**BBML** be back much later
AFAIK as far as I know	**BBN** bye bye now
AFK away from keyboard	**BBS** be back soon
AFN that's all for now	**BBSL** be back sooner or later
AKA also known as	**BCNU** I'll be seeing you
AISI as I see it	**BD** big deal
ALOL actually laughing out loud	**BEG** big evil grin
AND any day now	**BF** boyfriend
AOTA all of the above	**BFF** best friends forever
ASAP as soon as possible	**BFN** bye for now
AYSOS are you stupid or something	**BG** big grin
AYTMTB and you are telling me this because	**BIOYN** blow it out your nose
B4 before	**BKA** better known as
B4N bye for now	**BL** belly laughing
BAG busting a gut	**BR** best regards

Combat: Group Activity
Threat Level Assessment

Low-Risk

You're on a Group Chat when someone says something mildly negative or makes you feel left out. For example: "im not talking to u, im talking to her," or "I don't care, that's stupid." What do you do?

_____

_____

_____

_____

_____

_____

_____

Guarded Risk

You're on a Group Chat with several people and someone starts saying rude or mean things to you. Everybody joins in using flaming, harassment, or exclusion. The language is more sharp and cruel, uses profanity, and/or would violate the terms of your school's online rules. What do you do?

_____

_____

_____

_____

_____

_____

_____

Elevated Risk

The Group Chat conversation turns into a serious Digital Pile On with multiple people joining as a gang of bullies. The language becomes abusive, and people are swearing or posting your personal info (email address, phone number) to encourage more abuse from followers on the buddy list. What do you do?

_____

_____

_____

_____

_____

_____

_____

High-Risk

The bullies encourage others to post "hate speech" (any words that disrespect your race, gender, disability, sexual orientation) or make statements to provoke other unknown people to stalk and harass you or post threatening comments saying you will be hurt or killed. What do you do?

_____

_____

_____

_____

_____

_____

_____

Internet Tactics: Rating Website

Rating Website:

A website that encourages people to rate or vote on the attractiveness of the people in the uploaded photos.

With this tactic, the target either uploads a photo of himself to a rating website or a bully posts an unflattering photo of the target without his or her knowledge. The bully and other **downraters** proceed to negatively rate the target's attractiveness for the purpose of entertainment or revenge.

Getting Started

Lesson Rundown   Students are introduced to the concept of a common tactic called a Rating Website, in which students vote online to negatively rate the attributes of another student.

Objective   Students will be able to:

- understand what a Rating Website is and how it is used to cyberbully;
- make deliberate choices to avoid a Rating Website and be aware of the consequences of participating in one;
- assess how to defend themselves ethically and legally in escalating situations;
- practice examining the bully's motives and remain in control in the aftermath of a Rating Website.

Time Needed   The Understand, Combat, and Transform sections are structured to be conducted within a typical classroom requiring 30-40 minutes of lesson time. The Prevent sections may require 30-60 minutes as they go more in-depth and may prompt more conversation. Total estimated time for the Rating Website Unit is 2-3 hours, and will vary in an after-school or workshop environment.

Teacher Prep   Review any group or individual activities ahead of time for materials needed to maximize in-class time.

Equipment/ Supplies Needed   Computers with Internet access can be used for high-tech activities. Otherwise, paper and writing materials can be used for low-tech activities.

Vocab Words   Defined at the end of this section.

Handouts   *Group Activity, "My Worst Secret Is" Threat Level Assessments*

For The Educator

Tactic Overview

Our goal is to educate teachers and students how a Rating Website works and how this particular form of entertainment can cause emotional trauma to a teen's developing self-image. This chapter will convey why participating in a Rating Website is bullying and underscores the personal costs that come with negatively rating another. You will be able to teach students how to protect themselves online and what to do if they have been a target of a Rating Website. Students who've never seen a Rating Website may be tempted to use one out of curiosity, which is to be expected, but by the end of this chapter, they will understand the consequences of participating in one.

How A Rating Website Is Used: Although the practice of rating the physical attractiveness of people has been around for hundreds of years, this generation of kids growing up today are immersed in **tabloid culture**, in which the faces and bodies of celebrities are endlessly scrutinized by the online media, in reality shows, and in the tabloid magazines at the grocery check-out counter. Combine this with the self-conscious adolescent need to self-assess and compare themselves to others on a Rating Website and you've got a built-in online bullying tool. A Rating Website is designed to be a fun time-waster for users to vote on or **rate** people, content, or other things. The website is typically organized around physical appearance, body parts, voice, personality, etc. Users score items on a scale of 1 to 10, yes or no. Then, those statistics are aggregated into "best" and "worst" lists.[51]

As an interesting aside, Mark Zuckerberg, the founder of Facebook, actually started his career by building a version of a Rating Website in his college years. His original Harvard project called "Facemash" compared female Harvard students to each other and let users vote on which one was more attractive.[52]

With a still-developing sense of **empathy**, some teens just don't understand why rating someone for a "worst" list isn't funny. With Rating Websites, the level of anonymity is high. A user can join a Rating Website community with a **pseudonym** and thus be shielded from the target knowing his or her real identity. Rating Websites usually provide some features of social network services and online communities such as discussion forums messaging and private messaging.[53] This also fulfills a need to "belong" to an online group where members can feel superior to those they rate.

Scenario
Stephen's Story

Print the below story and hand out to the students. For more interactivity, assign someone to read it to the entire class.

Brotherly Love: On a Scale of 1–10

Joe, seventeen, had gotten home from school before his younger brother Stephen, fifteen. While waiting for a mini pizza to heat up in the oven, Joe got online to check his favorite site, www.ratemybody.com. This site cracked him up. There were so many ugly people who thought they were hot! He liked to see who was new and rate their looks from 1–10. He liked this site more than others because under each photo was a bio as well as a comment section that let others rate the photo in public. If a girl really seemed stuck up in her bio, he'd give her photo an automatic 1, just to mess with her. He continued to cruise the site just as Stephen came through the apartment door. Suddenly, Joe got a brilliant idea—it would be so funny to post a photo of Stephen up on the site and then get all of his friends to rate him as a "1" or a "0" and then blast him in the comments section. He opened up a computer file of photos his mother recently took of them both. Joe knew exactly the one he wanted to find: a headshot of Stephen with a dumb look on his face, made even funnier by his ball cap tipped off center. The best part? Stephen had a cold sore on his lower lip.

Joe quickly set up a fake account under Stephen's name. Immediately, he emailed his friends to go to the site, rate Stephen, and post comments. Joseph couldn't stop laughing to himself. This was probably the best prank he'd pulled off in a while. Within an hour, Joe checked back on the rating site. There were thirty of the most mean and nasty comments rating not just Stephen's photo, but also his clothing, his face, even his Italian heritage. *Wow, this is really harsh,* Joe thought, frowning as he read through the comments. This was supposed to be a funny prank, but the comments people were leaving were way meaner than he expected. Who were these people? All the comments were under anonymous screen names, so it was hard to know who was an actual friend and who wasn't. Joe expected people to make fun of Stephen, but not throw so much hate his way. Joe suddenly felt very uneasy and deleted the fake account. He decided not to tell Stephen about the prank after all. If Stephen saw any of the comments, he wouldn't take it as a joke. He hoped not too many people had seen it.

The next day, Stephen came up to Chelia, a girl he liked, in the hallway. At that moment, one of Chelia's friends walking by called over her shoulder: "Hey, Stephen, you need to get that thing on your lip taken care of." Chelia seemed embarrassed for him as Stephen stared at her friend, confused. As he walked away from Chelia, his fists clenched. He could feel his face become hot. Why did Chelia's friend say that, making him look like a fool? At lunch, Stephen's friend told him he'd seen the www.ratemybody.com site and that people were saying awful things about him. When Stephen got a chance, he used his phone to get online and find the Rating Website about him, but couldn't find the profile. Then, as he got on Facebook, he went cold. He discovered his own photo—the one his mom took last month with the embarrassing cold sore at the corner of his mouth. It was now circulating around everyone's Facebook news feeds like wildfire. From the comments on Facebook, Stephen could tell this photo had been lifted from the now-deleted Rating Website, but that everyone now had a copy of it. He knew his brother was the only one who would've had that photo. After reading the meanest, ugliest comments anyone had ever said about him, he felt himself begin to tremble. The fact that his *brother* had done this, turning him into a punching bag online, embarrassing him in front of Chelia, was unbelievable!

When Stephen got home that day, there was Joe, as usual, on the computer. Before his brother had even turned around to look at him, Stephen shoved Joe to the floor. Then, in a rage, Stephen swept the laptop to the floor as well, snapping the screen off and breaking it into pieces.

"I didn't mean it," Joe yelled, his hands covering his face. "Stephen, believe me! It was only supposed to be a joke!"

Step I: Understand

Objective	Students will be able to:
	• identify with the roles of a bully, follower, or a defender;
	• identify one's deeper motivations/needs for participating in a Rating Website;
	• understand the concept of empathy with respect to using a Rating Website.
Time Needed	55 minutes.
Teacher Prep	Read any passage ahead of class time labeled "For the Educator."
Equipment/ Supplies Needed	Copier. Computers with Internet access (high-tech) or paper and pencils (low-tech).
Vocab Words	Defined at the end of this section.

Overview

Start with the Topic for Discussion to get students warmed up. Gradually move on to show them the various roles people play in this particular tactic.

Establish Group Guidelines	See the guidelines in **Appendix C** in order to get the most out of your group discussions in class.

Rating Websites
www.Hotornot.com
www.Ratemybody.com
www.Ratemyface.com
www.Cuteornot.com
www.Meoryou.com

Topic for Discussion   Many students admit that they use tech gadgets to "prank" each other because it's fun and easy to do, given the anonymity afforded the user. At the same time, many of these students don't even think what they're doing is cyberbullying. What other pranks do your students know of that have started on the Internet but soon turned ugly? Ask your students to identify who is the victim and who is the bully in this scenario. Then ask if there are other roles people have played, and identify them.

Define Tactic   Define what a Rating Website is. Ask your students if they've ever participated in one without knowing how it might affect others.

For The Student: A   Online conflict isn't always clear-cut. Once you've gotten through
Broader Perspective   the Topic For Discussion, summarize for your students the actual roles of each participant as outlined below.

From The Bully's Perspective: Pranks among friends and siblings will always occur, but with the Internet, pranks like this can jump offline and have even more unintended consequences. Joe didn't have enough compassion to foresee the kind of humiliation his brother would experience both online and off. He hadn't set up Stephen's photo on the Rating Website out of anger or revenge. He'd done it because he was just fooling around and thought it would be fun. He even thought Stephen would get a laugh out of it too . . . until the prank got out of control. It didn't occur to Joe that what he did would result in a broken laptop computer and a destroyed relationship with his brother.

From The Target's Perspective: Unlike someone who wanted to upload his own photo on a Rating Website (hoping, of course, to be widely rated as "hot"), Stephen was completely blindsided by this tactic. Like a lot of cyberbullying tactics, this one went viral (onto a different social media platform) and spilled into real life. After Chelia, the girl he really liked, had seen the site and was embarrassed for him, Stephen saw absolutely no humor in the prank. Would anyone? It took several weeks for this prank to stop entertaining the kids in his high school. He didn't talk to his brother for a month either, unable to forgive Joe.

From The Followers' Perspective: Joe's friends all became cyberbullying **followers** when they agreed to participate in this prank. While they thought they were being funny and adding comments meant to tease Stephen, in fact, **disinhibition** caused the **downraters** to add more and more mean comments just to outdo each other. Soon, strangers began to lash out at Stephen in sort of a **herd mentality**. Everyone lost sight of how it would affect Stephen once he read those comments. These followers also thought they were being funny, yet not one of them wanted the same thing to happen to them.

From The Passive Supporters' Perspective: By its very nature, Rating Websites are set up to encourage passive supporters to view people's photos for entertainment. Some of the kids at Stephen's school had a hard time believing that just by clicking through and viewing Stephen's photo on a Rating Website made them **accomplices** to cyberbullying, but that's the point. All a cyberbully needs is an audience. Whether students realize it or not, a **passive supporter** is anyone who willingly participates in viewing anything the cyberbully posts; doing so helps the bully, never the target.

Group Activity   Copy the Group Activity Scenario "My Worst Secret Is. . ." at the end of this chapter. Break students off into small groups and ask them to read the scenario as a group. Have them discuss the questions. Tell them at first glance her role may seem obvious, but to examine the root cause of her behavior a little deeper. Then each group may read their answers aloud to the class.

Teacher   Most times when kids sign up for a Rating Website, they have no
Takeaway Tip   idea they are giving away all of their rights to their photos by clicking "I agree" to the website's terms of service. For example, the website Rate My Body states: *By providing your image or picture to RMB, you grant RMB and RMB's users the worldwide, perpetual, and irrevocable right to make copies, or to authorize others to make copies of your image or picture, under the conditions set out in the preceding paragraph.*[54] Ask your students: what can happen when you give away all of your rights to your own image just by uploading it?

VOCAB WORDS

Accomplice: A person who joins with another in carrying out some plan (especially an unethical or illegal plan).

Disinhibition: Unrestrained behavior resulting from a lessening or loss of inhibitions or a disregard of cultural constraints.

Downraters: People online who rate or vote on something to make it lower in value, standard, or importance.

Empathy: The capability to share another being's emotions and feelings.

Followers: People who don't start the bullying, but join in and have the potential to escalate it.

Herd Mentality: A fear-based reaction to peer pressure which makes individuals behave all alike in order to avoid feeling "left behind" from the group.

Passive Supporters: Those who agree with the bullying, but don't take any active part in supporting the incident.

Pseudonym: A fictitious name used by a person to conceal his or her identity.

Step II: Prevent

Objective   Students will be able to:
- identify one's emotional state during conflict;
- analyze the underlying reasons for participating in a Rating Website;
- protect themselves with behavioral and technological strategies to prevent being the target of a Rating Website.

Time Needed   30-60 minutes.

Teacher Prep   Go over conflict resolution concepts with the class. For the group activity, you will need two pads of paper and pencils for each small group of 5–6 students.

Equipment/ Supplies Needed   A computer lab and printer would be beneficial for this section, but the individual and group activities can both be done in low-tech classrooms.

Vocab Words   Defined at the end of this section.

For The Educator: Conflict Resolution Concepts

Concepts to introduce to the class before we get into this section are about individual motivation and self-awareness. Very often, kids who have fights or disagreements don't even understand the underlying reasons. While analyzing the root causes of conflict are much broader and more complex than we can fully list in this section, we will touch upon two concepts:

Identifying Emotions and Understanding Individual Behavior

As stated in the first chapter, conflict typically occurs when one person's needs are thwarted by another. Joe is like millions of other teens, using the Internet to play out relationship issues without having any clear understanding of how his actions can cause harm to others. To get students to understand their needs and what motivates them to act a certain way, we have to ask the right questions. Helping students recognize and communicate their emotions on a more sophisticated level than just "mad/sad/glad" gets them to recognize their own complex emotional state and learn how to recognize the physiological signs of conflict.[55] For example, with anger, the signals would be "hairs standing up on the neck, face, and suddenly feeling hot, clenched teeth, trembling, or general body tension; embarrassment may be signaled by a general warming of the face; nervousness or anxiety may be signaled by stirring in the stomach, sweaty palms, or dry mouth."[56]

Individual Activity   Allow students to search online the keywords "Plutchik's wheel of emotions" on Wikipedia or else print it out and make copies for the class.[57] Then ask each student to pick one positive emotion and one negative emotion and list a situation that caused him or her to feel one of these emotions recently. These do not need to be shared with the rest of the class. Ask students to pick one of the emotions they identified. Ask them to write down what they might have needed or wanted that caused them to feel that emotion.

Self-Defense   On the board, write down two columns: **Behavior** and **Tech Defense**. Ask your class to volunteer their own suggestions to prevent being the target of a Rating Website and follow up by presenting the strategies below.

Behavior

- **What Do You Really Want?**: Before uploading any of your own photos to a Rating Website, ask yourself what it is you really want by doing this? Is it acceptance? Attention? Escape from boredom? Consider you may get the opposite of what you really want when uploading your photo, so think of healthier alternatives to get what you want.

- **Pays To Be Paranoid**: All of your photos should pass the "Would I Be Embarrassed If This Photo Got Out?" test. Never take or send out photos of yourself or allow others to take photos that are embarrassing, inappropriate, overly sexualized . . . or even silly. Always remember in this technological age, one's photo in the wrong hands can change the content of the photo's meaning instantly.

- **Friend Pact**: Ask your friends to make a **"friend pact"** that no one will ever upload another's photo without permission. Tell them they should *always* ask you before uploading any photos of you and that you *never* give permission to post any photos that are negative or compromising. Always be on the watch for each other's photos on the Internet.

- **Avoid Rating Websites Altogether**: Unlike email, chat, and other communication tools, you don't need to be on a Rating Website. This is the simplest advice we can give to avoid being a target, a bully, and a bystander of this particular tactic.

Tech Defense

You can either list the following strategies on the board, or if you have access to a computer lab and additional time, some of these exercises can be easily done online in a class period. These suggestions and practice sessions will help students learn to recognize negative tactics and positive affirmations as well as take active roles as allies.

- **Do A Screen Capture**: If you ever discover your image on a Rating Website that was put up there without your permission and want to save it as proof, follow these steps. *For Windows Users*: Find and press the "Print Screen" key on the keyboard. It is usually labeled PrtScrn. This will copy an image of the screen into the Windows clipboard or desktop. Once captured, the screenshot must be pasted from the clipboard into a separate program, such as Paint or Word, in order to be viewed or saved. *For Macintosh Users (OS X)*: Press Command-Shift-3. Use the cursor to capture the entire screen and save it to your hard drive. Look for a file named Picture 1 (the number may change if you already have images saved in this manner).[58]

- **Create A Google Alert**: Each student should create a Google Alert with his or her real name and any nicknames. A Google Alert scours the web for any information with specific keywords the student plugs in and delivers the content back to the student via email. Consider adding additional words like HOT, NOT, UGLY, STUPID, etc. to strengthen this search. These alerts can then be sent to an email address of your choice, and you can also set how often (i.e. weekly, daily). So if someone has posted an image about a student, he or she will be the first to know.[59]

- **Watermark Your Image**: Using free, photo-altering applications like www.picmarkr.com, students may superimpose their social networking profile ID on top of their profile image as a watermark. Students will immediately know (and can inform others) if anyone misuses the original picture by posting it without the watermark.[60]

- **Monitor Your Profile**: Students need to be smart, not only in the type of photographic content they upload themselves, but especially what their friends take and post of them. Even with social profiles set to private, photos that you share with others can be posted publicly somewhere else—even if you delete them in your own profile. Technology is close to reaching a point where **facial recognition software** will be available to do a reverse image search for your own photo. And when that happens, Michael Fertik and David Thompson, authors of *Wild West 2.0*, warn, "a simple search for somebody's name will reveal tens (or hundreds) of photos of them. This is especially true for embarrassing photos of teenagers that have spread to a wide audience."[61] Have your students check their names with the reputation monitoring tool Social Mention, www.socialmention.com

- **UnTag/Hide Yourself**: With Facebook settings, you can click on Privacy Settings and customize "Photos and Videos I'm tagged in" to **untag** any photos you don't want your name under. This somewhat limits the controls others have in identifying your online images, but they can still upload a photo of you without your permission even if it is untagged. You can control who can see/use your profile photo by clicking on Privacy/Photos and customizing it to only be seen by you—and even hidden to people you don't want to have access to it.[62]

Group Activity   Break up the class into two groups. One group represents Joe. The other represents Stephen. Ask each group to take some time to answer the following questions. Then ask each group to act as an advocate for the brother they represent and "debate" with the other group about each brother could have handled their conflict better. Keep it friendly. Ask someone in the class to volunteer to write these suggestions down on the board or a flip chart.

Suggested Discussion Q's

Joe's Group

- What did Joe want out of this prank? What went wrong?
- What reaction could Joe have expected from Stephen before he put up that photo?
- How did Joe feel once he saw all those nasty comments about his brother?

Stephen's Group

- Was this conflict based on a misunderstanding? If so, whose?
- What bothered Stephen the most when he found out about the Rating Website?
- Violence was Stephen's first reaction. But if he'd been calmer, what would have been a better way to let Joe know what he did was wrong?

VOCAB WORDS

Facial Recognition Software: A computer application for automatically identifying or verifying a person from a digital image or a video frame.

Friend Pact: A formal agreement made and signed by two or more friends.

Identifying Emotions: Recognizing positive and negative emotions and identifying what is causing them.

Understanding Individual Behavior: Pinpointing what particular emotions you are feeling when you are in conflict.

Untag: Remove links to any photos of yourself online.

Step III: Combat

Objective

Students will be able to:

- identify low- to high-risk online situations;
- assess possible solutions to remedy conflict without resorting to revenge;
- practice making thoughtful, deliberate choices on how to react to the threat.

Time Needed

30 minutes.

Teacher Prep

Read any section ahead of class time labeled "For the Educator." Make a copy each of the Threat Level Assessments to hand out to four small groups.

Equipment/ Supplies Needed

Copier for handouts and pencils for students.

Vocab Words

Defined at the end of this section.

In the following section we use our own version of the US Department of Defense's concept of "Threat Levels" when providing students action steps to take.

Note: the advice in this section does not purport to be legal advice. We have consulted with cyberbullying experts to help parents and students know what to do in a Rating Website situation.

Immediate Steps To Take
First Step: Report Abuse

Most of the Rating Websites we looked at had an eighteen-and-over age requirement as well as a "terms of use" agreement in order to sign up. Though Rating Websites can't control if an underage teen chooses to sign up with fictitious information, most Rating Websites do require each user to agree to not invade someone's privacy, misrepresent an uploaded photo, and/or not to post anything defamatory, threatening, hateful, harassing, abusive, unlawful, vulgar, obscene, or harmful. To report abuse you can either click on a link under the photo that says "Report this" or contact the Rating Website directly. Locate the "Terms and Conditions" tab to find the email of the **Webmaster**.[63]

Second Step: Make screenshots

To prove what is being posted about the student before requesting the Webmaster to take the photo down, refer to Tech Defense above to take a **screenshot** of a website on your computer. In extreme cases one will need a **subpoena** in order to find out who uploaded and posted the photo.

Threat Level Assessment

In this section, the group activity comes before the lesson. This allows students to "pre-play" how they might react to each escalating situation. *Educators will need to make copies of the four Threat Level Assessments at the end of this chapter before the group activity can begin.*

Group Activity   Split the class into four small groups and ask them to retreat to each corner of the room. Assign each group a hypothetical situation ranging from Low-Risk to High-Risk (handouts found at the end of this chapter). Appoint a group leader to read the Threat Assessment on each handout to the group, and give each group a chance to write down their solutions to each hypothetical situation. After each group is done, ask the group leader (starting with Low-Risk) to read the group's suggestions out loud to the class. Educators can provide the correct answer from the "What To Do" guide below for each Threat Level.

1. **Low-Risk**: You upload your photo willingly to a Rating Website, hoping people will make nice comments about you; however, you are surprised to see some mild but negative comments.

   Frequency: It happens once.

   What To Do: You can at any time delete your photo or request the Webmaster of the Rating Website to take it off the website. If you see anything that makes you upset or uncomfortable, do this right away. It's not worth it to keep the photo up. Do not try to defend yourself in the comments section or you'll encourage even more negative comments.

2. **Guarded Risk**: You find out a photo of you taken by someone else was uploaded to a Rating Website. Mean and unfair comments about your image are being made by a group of people you're not sure you know.

   Frequency: It happens once, but it's been up there for a while before you discover it.

   What To Do: First make a **screen shot** of the Rating Website. If someone else took your photo, that person technically *owns* the rights to that photo (even if it's you); however, under most terms of service, the user is forbidden from posting a photo that is intended to harass and abuse another person. Therefore, report abuse of the photo to the Webmaster of the Rating Website with a "request for removal." Tell the Webmaster that the photo is being misrepresented for the purpose of **harassment** and **defamation** and is invading your privacy. (Use these words exactly.)

   We suggest you tell your parents or a trusted adult at this point, because even if the photo of you is taken down, someone still owns the rights to it and may put it wherever they like. Your parents may have to talk with an attorney if you are harassed any more.

3. **Elevated Risk**: You shared your photo with others on your own social networking profile and now it has been copied and **Photoshopped** by someone you don't know to ridicule you and has been uploaded to a Rating Website. Comments on the website are getting abusive or revealing your personal info (email address, cell number, passwords).

    Frequency: This happens once and it has not been taken down.

    What To Do: Even if this happens once, get screen captures/screenshots and either print them out or have a trusted adult print them out as soon as possible. Report abuse to the Webmaster and show the saved proof to your parents and/or school administrators right away, especially if you think this happened at school or it might be someone at school doing this.

4. **High-Risk**: A person takes and uploads your photo and encourages others to post "**hate speech**" (any words targeting race, gender, disability) under your photo, or makes statements to get others to stalk and harass you, or posts threatening comments to the Rating Website saying that you will be hurt or killed.

    Frequency: It has already happened and has not been taken down.

    What To Do: Have your parents or a trusted adult contact the police with all of your saved screen shots, because language like this immediately becomes a criminal issue. Most Rating Websites have protected themselves from any liability, even if the poster of the photo has stolen or misrepresented himself as owning or having rights to post the photo. But that doesn't mean the poster can't be subjected to legal action. The more the abuse fits the scenario mentioned above, the more help you and your parents will get from law enforcement.

Topic For Discussion Now that everyone has had a chance to see how much damage can be done on a Rating Website, ask your students to be truthful. Will they try going to a Rating Website now that they know what one is? (You should expect some will still say yes.) Ask them: "Can you put yourselves in the shoes of the person being made fun of?"

VOCAB WORDS

Defamation: Act of injuring another's reputation by any slanderous communication, written or oral.

Harassment: Behavior intended to disturb or upset or which is meant to threaten or disturb someone.

Hate Speech: Speech not protected by the First Amendment, because it is intended to foster hatred against individuals or groups based on race, religion, gender, sexual preference, place of national origin, or other improper classification.

Photoshopped: A technique of changing around a photo with colors, brushes, layers, etc., using the Photoshop program.

Screenshot: A screenshot or screen capture is an image taken by the computer to record the visible items displayed on the monitor.

Subpoena: A legal document that commands the recipient to produce evidence necessary to the resolution of a legal matter or controversy.

Webmaster: An employee of the organization that is hosting the website you need to contact.

Step IV: Transform

Objective:	Students will be able to:

- empathize with those who have been humiliated by a Rating Website by putting themselves in the target's shoes;
- practice making thoughtful, deliberate choices on how to react after the threat;
- "pre-play" how they would deal with being targets of a Rating Website if it happened to them.

Time Needed	30 minutes.
Teacher Prep	Allow students to read this section by themselves. For younger students, translate the concepts for better understanding.
Equipment/ Supplies Needed	Paper and pencils for students to take notes during Topic for Discussion.
Teacher Tip	This section is best absorbed if read first by the educator and used as a basis for a Topic For Discussion at the end.

Note: The Transform section is meant for the students to read on their own, as this is our advice to them directly. Present this as an in-class reading or a take-home reading assignment, and then come back as a class and introduce the Topic For Discussion. For younger students, educators might want to translate some of these concepts.

For The Student: The Damage Is Done, How To Cope

Martial artist and bullying counselor Chuck Nguyen says by the time we get to adulthood, we've had enough life experience to be able to overcome what someone else says about our appearance or imagined characteristics. But for teens, the emotional reaction to being rated negatively can be devastating. Trying to step back and keep control after something like this is incredibly difficult. But it is exactly what you need to do to transform the experience.

First Step: Examine Motives

Nothing is more hurtful than being humiliated by friends and strangers anonymously online about your physical appearance, your emotions, and your most intimate thoughts and dreams. Most students would easily identify with Stephen in this scenario. But it takes some cooling down emotionally and a clearer head to empathize with Joe and the unfortunate mistake he made by "pranking" his brother in such a humiliating way. Joe was clearly not out to deliberately hurt Stephen. He actually felt guilty and anxious afterward and did try to take the Rating Website profile down. It takes **empathy** to realize both brothers suffered significantly here. Stephen's suffering was emotional and social. Joe's was not only physical, but emotional as well.

In cyberbullying, the bully who feels remorse will often say, "I didn't mean to hurt him!" or, "I had no idea it would go this far!" And yes—it's harder to empathize with the one who did the damage. Getting the bully to understand what he or she did wrong is the most effective way of ending harm and hurt in the cycle of bullying—and may be the only chance to end the behavior. In situations like this scenario, when someone like Joe becomes a bully just by not knowing the motivations behind his actions, we must empathize with him and teach him to recognize **remorse** as a powerful behavioral tool.

Second Step: Stay In Control

In Martial Arts training, Chuck spends much of his time teaching students that ultimately, our enemy *is not somebody else*. The true enemy of your happiness is allowing your anger and obsessive negative thoughts to take over. When you are hurt, it's natural to want to "pay someone back." But this is the time to calm down and tap into your inner strength. When our natural tendency wants to take action in forms of violence and destruction—this is the time you must be stronger than your own emotions. You actually need to find more strength, more reserve, and more maturity than the bully—and this is how you demonstrate you are stronger. Of course, this option takes much more thought, insight, and self-control than hauling off and punching someone in the face, but retaliation will only cause more hurt and harm. If you go after the bully with **vengeance** or with violence, it doesn't teach someone what he or she did was wrong. It just perpetuates the conflict and motivates the bully to find deeper ways to hurt you back again. The suffering you have endured will have meaning because you have effectively and courageously faced your fears, emotions, and your opponents. In the end, in mastering your self-control, you will always win.

Third Step: Find A Good Listener

If you've been hurt or embarrassed by someone's unfair analysis of you on a Rating Website, don't "suck it up" and keep it to yourself. The only way to make it better is to tell a trusted friend or an adult. Otherwise, without getting an accurate read on what people value about you, you'll be stuck in this negative self-bashing loop, forever-wondering, "Why did they pick on me? Am I truly the way they view me?" This will not help you move forward and it will continue to lower your sense of self when right now you need to be working on building that up. Joining a safe, moderated cyberbullying support group or a Civil Rights team in your school will help you understand that you are not the only one this has happened to. In time, the support you get from your core friends and family will help you through the bad feelings you've suffered over this tactic.

Topic For Discussion   Now that you've been asked in this chapter to examine your own needs and motivations as well as your enemy's needs and motivations, how do you avoid feeling judged not just on a Rating Website, but in real life?

VOCAB WORDS

Empathy: The capability to share another being's emotions and feelings.
Remorse: An emotional expression of personal regret felt when someone has done something they realize is shameful, hurtful, or violent.
Vengeance: The act of taking revenge.

Rating Website Handouts
Understand: Group Activity

Break students off into small groups and ask them to read the scenario as a group. Have them discuss the questions below.

> **My Worst Secret Is** . . .
>
> I go on to a lot of online dating sites and I talk to a ton of guys. They love me because I will always reply to their emails and flirt back with them . . . I always have a ton of pictures on there so they feel safe that I am the girl they are talking to and will even send other ones not on the site if they ask for more, so they think I'm real. I have an endless supply of pictures because I actually use my friends' pictures that I take from Facebook and MySpace. I haven't had a problem yet. It's great. The boys always like to send me gifts and bribe me with trips to come see them. I always play it off like I'm busy with work and school, but tell them I have a birthday coming up; so every week I usually get some flowers or some type of gift from the guys. I know someday I will get caught, but until then, I love all the attention I'm getting. I feel so good about myself when I see that I have 20–50 messages a night from guys wanting to meet me and talk to me. It's hard for a lonely girl in the big city and this is a safe way for me to flirt with guys without people judging me for what I really look like.[64]

Define her "role":

☐ She is a target in this scenario

☐ She is a bully in this scenario

How did your group decide what this girl's role was in this scenario? List your reasons, explaining why: Target or Bully?

_____

_____

_____

_____

_____

53

Now that you've had a chance to read what this girl's "Worst Secret" is, discuss and answer the following questions as a group.

Despite what you think about her actions, what do you think this girl's hidden needs really are? In other words, what does she desperately want?

_____

_____

_____

_____

_____

_____

What would be a better and more honest way of meeting her needs without posting fake photos on these sites?

_____

_____

_____

_____

_____

_____

Combat: Group Activity
Threat Level Assessment

Low-Risk

You upload your photo willingly to a Rating Website, hoping people will make nice comments about you; however, you are surprised to see some mild but negative comments. What do you do?

_____

_____

_____

_____

_____

_____

_____

Guarded Risk

You find out a photo of you taken by someone else was uploaded to a Rating Website. Mean and unfair comments about your image are being made by a group of people you're not sure you know. What do you do?

_____

_____

_____

_____

_____

_____

_____

Elevated Risk

You shared your photo with others on your own social networking profile and now it has been copied and Photoshopped by someone you don't know to ridicule you and has been uploaded to a Rating Website. Comments on the site are getting abusive or revealing your personal info (email address, cell number, passwords). What do you do?

_____

_____

_____

_____

_____

_____

_____

High-Risk

A person takes and uploads your photo and encourages others to post "hate speech" (any words targeting race, gender, disability) under your photo, or makes statements to get others to stalk and harass you, or posts threatening comments to the Rating Website saying that you will be hurt or killed. What do you do?

_____

_____

_____

_____

_____

_____

_____

Internet Tactics: Imposter Profile

Additionally, you may report this profile as the following:

○ My friend is annoying me

◉ This profile is pretending to be someone or is fake

Pretending to be me ▾

| Choose a type |
| Pretending to be me |
| Pretending to be someone I know |
| Pretending to be a celebrity |
| Represents a business or an organization |
| Does not represent a real person |

Is this your intellectual property?   **Continue** Cancel

Imposter Profile:

An imposter is a person who makes deceitful pretenses. Syn: Fake, Fraud, Pretender.

With this tactic, a bully creates a fake social networking profile or website to deceive others into believing that it is genuinely owned and maintained by the target. The profile or website provides humiliating, false, and incriminating information about the target and/or secret disclosures, as if the target were willingly "confessing" this information.

Getting Started

Lesson Rundown

Students are introduced to the concept of the Imposter Profile, which is a deceptive website or social networking profile designed to lead others to believe it is genuinely owned and maintained by the target.

Objective

Students will be able to:

- understand what unintended messages their social networking profile communicates to others;
- make deliberate choices to portray themselves positively online;
- recognize the motivations behind escalating conflict;
- internalize the concept of being resilient after this tactic.

Time Needed

The Understand, Combat, and Transform sections are structured to be conducted within a typical classroom requiring 30-40 minutes of lesson time. The Prevent sections may require 30-60 minutes as they go more in-depth and may prompt more conversation. Total estimated time for the Imposter Profile Unit is 2–3 hours and will vary in an after-school or workshop environment.

Teacher Prep

Review any group or individual activities ahead of time for materials needed to maximize in-class time.

Equipment/ Supplies Needed

Computers with Internet access can be used for high-tech activities. Otherwise, paper and writing materials can be used for low-tech activities.

Vocab Words

Defined at the end of this section.

Handouts:

Threat Level Assessments

For The Educator

Tactic Overview

This chapter examines why an Imposter Profile is set up, how it's done, who participates, and ways to help students avoid one. This lesson will help your students understand that what they unwittingly put out as information about themselves on the Internet can always be used against them. You will be able to teach them how to protect themselves against an Imposter Profile by being proactive about their personal information while anticipating potential conflict.

How An Imposter Profile Is Made: An Imposter Profile is created by an individual who steals another person's identity or invents a nonexistent one to communicate a deceptive message. An AP-MTV study discovered "More than 1 in 10 have been the victim of impersonation, either by someone logging into their profile without permission (12%) or by someone making a fake profile (6%).[65] Sometimes a "friend" will create an Imposter Profile as a prank. Other times the intent is just malicious. The bully uses social technology to persuade others to believe that the target is projecting himself or herself in an unflattering way. The bully can also impersonate the target online to say derogatory things about others in order to embarrass the target or to get him or her in trouble. There is a lot of damage that can be done to the target's reputation with an Imposter Profile. Note: we've chosen Facebook and MySpace for the examples in this chapter, although a bully can pretend to be the target on any number of social media platforms, such as on websites, chat rooms, forums, or even in comments to someone's online posts. All a bully really needs is the target's personal information (or other information that is often readily available on the Internet), as well as access to secret passwords.

Scenario
Jake & Stephanie's Story

Print the below story and hand out to the students. For more interactivity, assign someone to read it to the entire class.

Digital Revenge

Friday, heading into school, Stephanie searched for Jake in the hallways, the cafeteria, even the library. She'd been texting him since last night, but he hadn't answered his phone. Psyched about going to their first dance together Saturday night, she needed to run some details by him about the limo all their friends were sharing. Finally, spotting him before first period, she tiptoed up to him and tugged on his shirt to say hi. Her smile faded as he avoided her eyes. After nagging him to admit what was wrong, Jake told her he just didn't want to go to the dance. Then he mumbled something about not wanting to even be in a relationship anymore and that he was sorry. Stunned, Stephanie couldn't even speak as she watched him walk away.

Desperate to understand what happened, Stephanie checked Jake's Facebook status on her iPhone at lunch. His relationship status had already been set to "Single" and she'd already been unfriended. The pain in her chest made her feel like she'd explode. They'd been together for three months and things had been going so well! What Jake did was so unexpected; it felt like she'd just been stabbed in the heart with a knife.

That Saturday night was the worst night of her life. While all of her friends were at the dance, Stephanie wiped away her tears and got on Facebook to find someone—anyone–to talk to. That's when she saw that Jake's last girlfriend, Rebekah, had commented on a mutual friend's post. She'd never been Facebook friends with Rebekah for obvious reasons before, but now Stephanie had nothing to lose. She sent a friend request to Rebekah. To her surprise and relief, Rebekah accepted her request immediately. As they went to Facebook's instant messaging feature to chat, Stephanie told Rebekah that Jake had broken up with her. Rebekah responded willingly about her own painful breakup with Jake, and after chatting further, they both realized they had a lot in common. That gave Stephanie a great idea—there was a way they could both get back at him. She confided her plan to Rebekah. They both knew Jake had a Facebook profile but he didn't have one on MySpace, so Stephanie quickly set up a MySpace account under his real name. At first glance, the social profile seemed genuine. Rebekah was still Facebook friends with Jake, so she lifted his bio on his real Facebook profile and copied and pasted it into the fake MySpace profile. Then, Stephanie altered a couple of old photos of Jake in Photoshop to make it look as though he was smoking a cigarette on school grounds and uploaded it to his new profile. She knew if any school administrators saw this, Jake would be sure to get kicked off the track team. On his "About me" profile, they listed his favorite color as "pink," listed some girly bands as his favorite music, and made a "true confession" in his own words that the reason he'd broken up with Stephanie was so he could steal another guy's girlfriend at school. Stephanie had never felt closer to anyone that night than Rebekah as they both giggled about what they'd done. Anonymously, they planned to send the imposter MySpace profile link to as many people as they knew at school.

By Monday, several dozen people at school had seen the imposter MySpace profile. Everyone thought it was real. It didn't take long for Jake to get threatened by a bunch of guys who really thought he was trying to steal their friend's girlfriend. At the end of school that day, someone slashed the tires on Jake's truck. When Stephanie heard that, she immediately texted Rebekah. "He had it coming," she typed.

Step I: Understand

Objective   Students will be able to:
- identify with the roles of a bully, follower;
- understand the emotional motivation for starting an Imposter Profile;
- analyze what the information on their social networking profile communicates to others.

Time Needed   55 minutes.

Teacher Prep   Copy handouts of the Scenario for the class.

Equipment/   Copier. Computers with Internet access (high-tech) or paper and
Supplies Needed   pencils (low-tech).

Vocab Words   Defined at the end of this section.

Overview

Start with the Topic for Discussion to get students warmed up. Gradually move on to show them the various roles people play in this particular tactic.

Establish Group   See the guidelines in **Appendix C** in order to get the most out of
Guidelines   your group discussions in class.

Topic for Discussion Ask students to identify who is the target and who is the bully in the above story. Are there other roles people have played? When everyone has had a chance to voice his or her observations, refer to below.

Define Tactic   Define an Imposter Profile. Ask students if they've ever seen one made about someone else and what they thought about it.

For The Student: Online conflict isn't always clear-cut. Once you've gotten through
A Broader Perspective the Topic For Discussion, go over the roles of each participant in the scenario with your class. We've provided multiple perspectives to help students gain insight.

From The Bully's Perspective: It's important to understand that Stephanie didn't wake up one morning and decide to be a bully. As a sixteen-year-old girl whose self-image was shaky, she was understandably upset with the way Jake had chosen to break up with her, but she reacted poorly by choosing to act as a social **vigilante**. Lacking maturity and **empathy**, she decided to make Jake "pay for what he'd done." **Public shaming** is a social practice that goes back to ancient communities and is a way for a group of people to feel morally superior to the person who has done wrong. When it jumps to the Internet, it gives the vigilante a feeling of social justice and power.

From The Target's Perspective: After Jake received threats from guys at school, he became immediately confused and worried. He didn't know what he'd done to make everyone so angry. He was already having a hard time after breaking up with Stephanie. She'd had high expectations of him and he didn't have the money to take her to the dance in a limo, just because all of her friends did. After discovering all four of his tires slashed (which was another $500 he didn't know how he was going to come up with), he received these disturbing texts that two guys were looking to beat him up. When he'd finally learned the source of all this trouble came from an imposter MySpace profile, he immediately guessed Stephanie was behind it and became very angry, but didn't know what to do next.

From The Follower's Perspective: Rebekah was initially surprised when Stephanie sent her a friend request, but when Stephanie told her how Jake had broken up with her, Rebekah remembered her own painful break up with Jake. The more she and Stephanie compared stories, the more motivated she was to help Stephanie get her revenge. To Rebekah, Jake deserved what was coming to him. She didn't feel bad about that MySpace profile because in her mind, she wasn't responsible for creating it—Stephanie was. Even though Rebekah didn't see herself as a bully, she was the classic definition of a follower: someone who doesn't start the bullying, but who plays an active role in helping it.

From The Passive Supporters' Perspective: All bullies need is an audience, and anyone who willingly participates is helping the bully. Of course, the dozens of kids at school who viewed the Imposter Profile probably didn't see themselves in that way, but they all took an active role, regardless. Most people don't think about it, but the moment you go from **lurking** on an Imposter Profile to actually posting a negative comment, you instantly switch from a passive supporter to the bully's **accomplice** as a follower.

Group Activity   The following activities use a website whose Internet Safety mission is to ward off predators, but for this lesson, ask students to look at it through the lens of how any information could be used against someone in an Imposter Profile.

High-tech: This exercise requires access to the Internet. Break students into groups of 3–4. Ask each group to go to this online "mock" profile that reveals too much information: http://www.komando.com/myspace/. Ask students to think like a bully and look for information that is considered too revealing and pick out any information that can be used against the target. What could be done to change the profile to minimize potentially negative information?

Low-tech: Ahead of time, take a screen shot of the mock profile in the above activity and print it off. (To see how, go to: Rating Website/Tech Defense/ "Practice a screen capture.") Ahead of time, review the answers that appear when you click the link at the bottom of the page. Break students into groups of 3–4. Ask students to think like a bully and look for information that is considered too revealing and pick out any information that can be used against the target. What could be done to change the profile to minimize potentially negative information?

Teacher   In our workshops with students and teachers, we often used the
Takeaway Tip   above activity as a way to show students exactly how vulnerable they are. In the eyes of an enemy, one's personal information can be turned into an embarrassing ordeal. Many students don't have the larger perspective that a social networking profile isn't just interesting to friends, it's highly interesting to enemies as well—all the more reason to teach them to be vigilant in protecting their privacy now. This group activity is more meaningful and powerful if you can get kids to view each other's social networking profiles (depending on how comfortable they are sharing it with others), to determine what information is too revealing and can be used against them.

VOCAB WORDS

Accomplice: A person who helps another in wrongdoing, or committing a crime.

Empathy: Identification with and understanding somebody else's situation, feelings, and motives.

Lurking: To read but not contribute to the discussion in a newsgroup, chat room, or other online forum.

Public Shaming: To cause someone to feel shame, a strong sense of guilt, embarrassment, unworthiness, or disgrace in public as a form of punishment.

Vigilante: One who punishes lawbreakers personally and illegally rather than relying on the legal authorities.

Step II: Prevent

Objective

Students will be able to:

- analyze the emotional factors that lead to cyberbullying;
- identify with both the bully's and the target's anger and examine the best plan of action;
- protect themselves with behavioral and technological strategies to prevent being the target of an Imposter Profile.

Time Needed

30-60 minutes.

Teacher Prep

Go over conflict resolution concepts with the class. For the group activity, you will need a small group of 5–6 students, a pen, and scrap paper.

Equipment/ Supplies Needed

A computer lab and printer would be beneficial for this section, but the individual and group activity can both be done in low-tech classrooms.

Vocab Words

Defined at the end of this section.

For The Educator: Conflict Resolution Concepts

Now that the students have identified the roles of bullies, targets, bystanders, and followers, it is time to "**post-play**" the opening scenario about Jake and Stephanie to get them to understand how to react in times of stress and anger. Introduce the conflict resolution concept to your class of **Analyzing Angry Emotions**.

According to Girard and Koch, authors of *Conflict Resolution in the Schools*, any time we experience anger it is due to fear. What happens is: 1) we perceive a threat to our needs; 2) the threat stimulates fear; and 3) the fear stimulates anger.[66] The first step to being responsible for our actions is to identify the fear underlying the anger. William J. Kreidler, author of *Conflict Resolution in Middle School*, came up with the concept **conflict escalator**. With each choice of behavior, conflict can escalate (step up) or de-escalate (step down). Each time you do something to make the situation worse, you move up one more step. The higher you go up the escalator, the harder it is to come down. As conflict escalates, so do intensity of emotions.[67] This is when people get violent or say and do things they regret. With intensity of emotions comes rash decisions when we post, click, or text under a highly emotional state.

Individual Activity   Ask your students to recall an incident or situation very recently that made them very angry, then write what happened down on a piece of paper. It doesn't have to be shown to anyone else. Underneath that, write the headings:

What I Did About It: List how they reacted, or if they even reacted at all.

Step Up: List one thing they might have done to make the conflict of the situation worse.

Step Down: List one thing they might have done to make the conflict of the situation better.

What Was The Threat/Fear?: Think about this carefully. Did the threat make them fear losing something? If so, what?

What I Wish I'd Done About It: Now, list whether they felt they made the right choice in that situation, or what they wish they'd done instead.

Self-Defense   On the board, write down two columns: **Behavior** and **Tech Defense**. Ask your class to volunteer their own suggestions to prevent being the target of an Imposter Profile and present the following strategies.

Behavior

- **1, 2, 3, Chill**: Your emotions are quick to make snap judgments, often irrationally, whenever you are angry or perceive a threat from someone. Always give yourself time to "cool off" before doing anything—especially if you are considering taking action online.

- **Identify Your Emotions**: "Triggers of past memories" can affect our perceptions, especially when something we experience in the present strongly reminds us of something negative that happened in our past. Analyze whether it is actually happening in the present or you are reacting to something from the past. If reacting from the past, you are not in immediate danger, but your mind *perceives* it as danger.[68]

- **Run It By A Friend**: When cooled off, check to see if your perceptions are "on target" or "off base," preferably with someone who witnessed the conflict.

- **Ditch The Drama**: Do not engage in any ongoing conflict online—don't even be a passive bystander to it! It gives the bully an audience.

- **Deal Face-To-Face**: If the conflict is with another person, deal with it in the real world. Ask the other person when he or she is alone and when you are both calm, if you can talk. If you need to, ask a teacher or a school mediator to help you **"pre-play"** this talk ahead of time and define what you want from the other person.

Tech Defense

You can either list the following strategies on the board, or if you have access to a computer lab (and additional time) some of these exercises can be easily done in a class period. These suggestions and practice sessions will help students learn to recognize negative tactics and positive affirmations, as well as take active roles as allies.

- **Create A Positive Profile**: Experts suggest you take control of your own identity online before someone else has the chance to do it. Whatever social utility the majority of students are using at your school (MySpace, Hi5, Facebook—this list will invariably change) ask your class to consider creating a social networking profile with positive information. In other words, take charge of your own public relations. (Depending on the student's age and parental policies, check with parents first.) Set your social networking profile account settings to be Private immediately—meaning it is only viewable by people you allow—and be very cautious about safekeeping your passwords and whom you accept as friends on your social profile.

- **The Super Log-Off And "White-walling" Techniques**: For Facebook users, The Super Log-Off refers to deactivating your account entirely each time you log out through your Account Settings page, then reactivating it when you log in. Facebook keeps your profile intact even when it is deactivated and it's a snap to reactivate it with no loss of information. When it is deactivated, no one can have access to or use anything on your Facebook account. White-walling means deleting every single wall post or status update within twenty-four hours, leaving what you post up just long enough for friends to see what you want them to see. Again, with White-walling, no one can have access to or use anything on your Facebook account.[69]

- **Disable All Unused Email Accounts**: Bullies can use unused email accounts if the target's passwords have been shared, so disable the ones you never use. Take the ones you do use and add them to your legitimate account (because if someone starts an Imposter Profile, you will be alerted when you get the confirmation email).[70]

- **Monitor Your Online Reputation**: Each student should create a **Google Alert** (see how to do this in Haters' Club/Tech Defense) or check his or her name and any nicknames through SocialMention at www.socialmention.com. These tools scour the web, blogs, forums, bookmarks, events, news, and videos for any keywords and deliver the content back to the student via email updates. So, if someone has posted something about you, you will be the first to know.

- **Redirect To Legitimate Site**: If an Imposter Profile crops up under the student's legitimate name, the student or a friend can leave <u>one</u> comment on the Imposter Profile announcing that it is a fake and direct people to the legitimate site. Don't say anything more on the Imposter Profile than that and don't go back to comment on it.

Group Activity   Ask your students to form two small groups, each representing Jake and Stephanie. Depending on the emotional maturity of your students, it would be interesting to try to have all the boys represent Stephanie and all of the girls represent Jake, but arrange the groups in a way that will encourage the most discussion. Ask your students to approach each question rationally, not emotionally, as there may be a strong gender bias toward the characters in this scenario.

Each group should come up with answers to the following questions. Ask someone in the group to volunteer to write the following answers down and be willing to share them with the class afterward.

Suggested Discussion Q's

From Jake's perspective:

- Do you think Jake knew what it was like to be in Stephanie's shoes over this conflict?
- Knowing Stephanie wanted to go to a dance in a style he couldn't afford, what else could he have done?
- No one likes to break up, but could he have done something different to let her down easier?
-

From Stephanie's perspective:

- What was Stephanie afraid of? What did she "lose" that turned her fear to anger?
- In which ways could Stephanie have communicated her hurt feelings to Jake without taking it out on him online?
- Did you think revenge was the best way to express anger?

VOCAB WORDS

Analyze Angry Emotions: Identifying the fear that is underlying our emotional angry reaction.

Conflict Escalator: A conflict escalator is something that causes a conflict to get more intense, more quickly.

Google Alert: A content monitoring service, offered by the search engine company Google, that automatically notifies users when new content from news, web, blogs, video, and/or discussion groups matches a set of search terms selected by the user.

Post-Play: In "role-playing" this means analyzing what happened in the game (or scenario) after it happens to know what to do in the event of a similar situation next time.

Pre-Play: In "role-playing" this means acting out the possible outcomes of the game (or scenario) before it happens.

The Super-Logoff: The practice of deactivating your Facebook account entirely each time you log out, then reactivating it when you log in to completely control who has access to your content.

White-Walling: Deleting every single wall post or status update within 24 hours, leaving what you post up just long enough for friends to see what you want them to see.

Step III: Combat

Objective
Students will be able to:
- identify low- to high-risk online situations;
- assess possible solutions to remedy conflict without resorting to revenge;
- practice making thoughtful, deliberate choices on how to react to the threat.

Time Needed
30 minutes.

Teacher Prep
Read any passage ahead of class time labeled "For the Educator." Make a copy of each of the Threat Level Assessments to hand out to four small groups.

Equipment/ Supplies Needed
Copier for handouts and pens/pencils for students.

Vocab Words
Defined at the end of this section.

In the following section we use our own version of the US Department of Defense's concept of "Threat Levels" when providing students action steps to take.

Note: *the advice in this section does not purport to be legal advice. We have consulted with cyberbullying experts to help parents, educators, and students know what to do in an Imposter Profile situation.*

Immediate Steps To Take
First Step: Report Abuse

There is a link at the bottom of most social networking profiles to report abuse.

For a social networking site like MySpace, you will see step-by-step instructions on how to do this by Googling "How To Remove an Imposter Profile." For Facebook, go to the help center and type in "fake profile." A help page will come up to instruct you on what to do. For other websites or blogs, find the "contact" form, and then open the fake profile in your browser and select Report Abuse Option in that profile.

Facebook, MySpace, and other social networking sites are often criticized for not responding quickly enough to online harassment. In some cases, people have gotten no response until the police become involved—so if the student is too frightened or unequipped to solve the problem alone, encourage the student to find someone (a parent, a trusted adult, a school counselor, a Civil Rights team, a school principal) who can effectively intervene.

Second Step: Fill out Scene Survey and Keep Evidence

Fill out as much detail in a **Scene Survey** (**Appendix B**) as possible, gathering facts, dates, and evidence. If the situation escalates, this starts the fact-based paper trail that parents, school administrators, Internet Service Providers, and possibly the police will need to see from the beginning.

Third Step: Do Your Own Sleuthing

Sometimes a student can do his or her own investigation based on the tools he or she already has. One target of an Imposter Profile tracked down a fake Gmail account set up in her name and clicked "Forgot Password." She easily guessed the answer to the security question Gmail posed, gained access to the email and Facebook accounts, and changed the passwords and security questions. From there she used a free IP (Internet Protocol) address tracker to track the network where the computer that was used to create the fake site was located.[71] All of this investigation led to arrests of the students who started the Imposter Profile.

Threat Level Assessment

In this section, the group activity comes before the lesson. This allows students to "pre-play" how they might react to each escalating situation. *Educators will need to make copies of the four Threat Level Assessments at the end of this chapter before the group activity can begin.*

Group Activity   Split the class into four small groups and ask them to retreat to each corner of the room. Assign each group a hypothetical situation ranging from Low-Risk to High-Risk (handouts found at the end of this chapter). Appoint a group leader to read the Threat Level Assessment on each handout to the group, and give each group a chance to write down their solutions to each hypothetical situation. After each group is done, ask the group leader (starting with Low-Risk) to read the group's suggestions out loud to the class. Educators can provide the correct answer from the "What To Do" guide below for each Threat Level.

1. **Low-Risk**: An Imposter Profile about you shows up, and statements about you are mildly annoying and/or embarrassing (but not cruel or excessive). The Imposter Profile shows no photos of you and no identifying information other than your name.

    Frequency: The website is up, but is not widely viewed by many people.

    What To Do: Any time a bully registers a website or social networking profile under another person's real name or pretends to be the person on the site, it is automatically a violation of the hosting website or service. The problem with an annoying, one-time incident like this is that one never knows how far it will go, so it is always best at the first instance to let parents, a trusted teacher, and/or school officials know about it right away. Contact the Imposter Profile's **Webmaster** or go to "Contact Us" or "Report Abuse" on the website. For mild cases, many times the website or social networking site will be too slow in responding; don't give up! Start collecting data using the **Scene Survey** (**Appendix B**) worksheet, and then provide the Webmaster with all the details, while sticking to the facts. It should take a few days or up to a week for it to be removed, but check back and make sure it is. While it is up, ignore it—don't ever comment on it yourself, because bullies thrive on their target's negative reactions and it motivates them to keep up the harassment.

2. **Guarded Risk**: The Imposter Profile shows up about you. You've already tried to get it shut it down and/or told a parent or teacher. The website still hasn't been taken down after a week and lots of people are starting to add to it or comment on it.

   Frequency: The profile/website continues to stay up despite warnings to remove it. Posts/comments from others are increasing.

   What To Do: Print out and preserve all evidence (**screenshots**, emails, IM **chat logs**) as soon as possible. Do this quickly because most evidence "disappears" once the bully knows you're taking action. At this stage, you should have already told a trusted adult. Notify the school authorities if you have any suspicions that it involves students from school. If they are making negative comments on school time, this falls under the school's cyberbullying policy. Create your own legitimate profile or website, and in a neutral tone state briefly and factually that the Imposter Profile is in the process of being shut down and all harassing comments are being saved for evidence. Put a comment with a link to your legitimate website on the Imposter Profile where people can go to find the truth.

   Take care in notifying the parents of the bully to stop the behavior. "Parents of the target may want to consider whether contacting the parents of the bully is more strategic if they do it personally or go through the police," says Seattle school attorney Thomas Hutton. "Where the parents of the bully may have no idea what is going on, just letting them know may be enough to resolve the situation. If you don't get the reaction you want, it may be time to up the ante. In some situations in which school officials question whether they have authority over off-campus cyberbullying, law enforcement authorities may have more leeway," adds Hutton, who notes that police or school resource officers sometimes have addressed cyberbullying by pointing out criminal laws such as those addressing harassment or identity theft. "Often a mere warning from law enforcement is enough to resolve the situation."[72]

3. **Elevated Risk**: The Imposter Profile shares personal information about you that threatens your reputation or repeatedly harasses you with very embarrassing information (whether or not the information is true) or posts obscene statements or lists your personal info (email address, cell phone number, address, where to find you alone, etc.).

Frequency: The website continues to stay up. Anonymous negative or cruel comments are increasing, causing you extreme emotional distress.

What To Do: At this level, some of the content on the Imposter Profile is crossing the boundaries of rudeness into criminal language.[73] Go straight to law enforcement with all of your saved screen shots and **Scene Survey (Appendix B)**. They will be able to locate the **Internet Service Provider ISP** of the Imposter Profile and need to be involved in order to **subpoena** the website provider to obtain information that may lead to the identification of the bully.

4. **High-Risk**: The bully behind the Imposter Profile gets a lot of people to post threatening comments about you (how they're going to hurt you) or "**hate speech**" comments (any words targeting your race, gender, disability, or sexual orientation) or says on the site that they are going to stalk and harass or kill you or tells you to kill yourself.

Frequency: The Imposter Profile still hasn't been taken down after several weeks or it has been shut down, but others are now being created about you and the harassment continues to happen offline because of it.

What To Do: Follow all of the steps above and continue to save all evidence, including screenshots, a **Scene Survey (Appendix B)**, subpoenas, and continue to work with law enforcement. The more the situation appears to pose a real danger of playing out at school, the stronger the school's discretion will be to intervene, even if the bullying up to that point has occurred only off-campus. Any time written language is being used to threaten someone or intentionally inflict emotional distress or torment, harass, humiliate, and embarrass the student, the more likely the student and his or her parents have a legal case against the bully. Consult an attorney with cyber crime experience at this level.

Topic For Discussion Ask your students where they draw the line over this type of harassment. In other words, at what point does one stop ignoring it and ask an adult to intervene?

VOCAB WORDS

Chat Logs: A log of an online chat between users.

Hate Speech: Speech not protected by the First Amendment, because it is intended to foster hatred against individuals or groups based on race, religion, gender, sexual preference, place of national origin, or other improper classification.

IP (Internet Protocol): The method or protocol by which data is sent from one computer to another on the Internet. Each computer (known as a host) on the Internet has at least one IP address that uniquely identifies it from all other computers on the Internet.

Screenshots: A screenshot or screen capture is an image taken by the computer to record the visible items displayed on the monitor.

Subpoena: A legal document that commands the recipient to produce evidence necessary to the resolution of a legal matter or controversy.

Webmaster: An employee of the organization that is hosting the website you need to contact.

Step IV: Transform

Objective

Students will be able to:

- empathize with those who have been attacked by putting themselves in the target's shoes;
- assess the advantages of being resilient in the aftermath of an attack;
- "pre-play" how they would deal with being targets of a Imposter Profile if it happened to them.

Time Needed

30 minutes.

Teacher Prep

Allow students to read this section by themselves. For younger students, translate the concepts for better understanding.

Equipment/ Supplies Needed

Paper and pencils for students to take notes during Topic for Discussion.

Note: The Transform section is meant for the students to read on their own, as this is our advice to them directly. Present this as an in-class reading or a take-home reading assignment, and then come back as a class and introduce the Topic For Discussion. For younger students, educators might want to translate some of these concepts.

For The Student: The Damage Is Done, How To Cope

This lesson is about transforming pain into pride. A student who has been cyberbullied, slammed, or **defamed** by an Imposter Profile can overcome it.

One of the most effective metaphors martial artist and bullying counselor Chuck Nguyen uses to teach his students is the image and quality of water and how to live and fight like it.

Be Like Water

Water can be gentle and insignificant, but with the right momentum and shift, water can be the most resilient, effective, and powerful form of energy. One of the factors that makes water powerful is what happens when it faces obstacles. Imagine a stream with lots of rocks and broken branches. What happens when these obstacles get in the path of a moving stream? Do they hold water back? No. Water becomes more powerful in the confrontation. The rocks are challenged gradually, smoothed over—the branches are swept away over time.

Chuck challenges students to practice this kind of mental flexibility after dealing with an Imposter Profile. The threat is not physical, but emotional. If we choose to approach how others can mistreat us effectively like water, we will become more powerful—not weakened—over time. We have to find new paths and possibilities to overcome the obstacles. This is not an easy fix. This is a daily struggle to channel the humiliation, shame, and stress that might come after an Imposter Profile the same way water channels itself around and over the hard rocks. It means enduring, finding, and believing the good within yourself, not giving up or giving in to violence and rage. At the same time, the most important thing a community of parents, friends, teachers, and neighbors—even strangers—can do, is reassure the target with positive messages, affirmations of their support, and encourage the target not to give in to feelings of worthlessness. To transform the lowered self-esteem from the effects of an Imposter Profile, you need to know this has happened to others, you are not alone, and this tactic is not unique to just young people. Those who have been injured by an Imposter Profile need to branch out, find more allies, discover new talents, or work toward new goals. We don't mean to make this sound like it is easy, because it is not. But it takes practice, patience, and endurance in order to create new paths in your life and new resources to keep working toward the best person you will eventually become.

Don't Be Like A Rock

Our only other choice in dealing with injustice in life is to be like a rock—hard on the surface, which can ultimately smash, explode, and crumble to nothingness. To many, revenge might *sound* more satisfying at first. You might hear kids say, "But why should I let the bullies get away with it?" If everyone has followed the steps in this chapter and has taken the proper action, it will make it very difficult for the cyberbullies to "get away" with it. During Chuck's counseling experience, he has met so many young people in the prison system who have made the choice of anger and **retaliation**. They defend their rights against injustice by being violent and hard like a rock. As a result, they end up becoming bullies themselves and learn nothing from their pain. They constantly live in anger and pain in the ineffective and harmful ways they choose to deal with being hurt. If we choose to react to the injustice of an Imposter Profile like a rock, we continue to harm ourselves after the incident by losing what might be the only thing left—our ability to move on, heal, and become stronger.

Now, *water or rock*—how does that apply to an Imposter Profile? Take Allison Pfeiffer, eighteen, a target of an Imposter Profile that referred to her as a cow (among other nasty names) with the intent to ridicule her. At first, she cried for several hours. Then, facing her pain head-on, she spent seven hours tracking down the digital trail that the creators of the Imposter Profile left behind as clues (see Combat: Third Step). "I'm not tech-savvy at all, but it actually wasn't that hard," says Pfieffer, whose sleuthing led the police to the two bullies (so-called friends) who claimed they were just bored and looking to entertain themselves. They were charged with **criminal impersonation**, second-degree harassment, conspiracy to commit criminal impersonation, and conspiracy to commit second-degree harassment. Now studying to be a lawyer, Pfeiffer says, "It actually did make me want to go to law school even more now, because I would love to fight for someone who found [herself] in my situation. Some of my friends would have hung themselves over this. So I'm just glad that [the bullies] got a stable person trying to take a positive approach to dealing with it rather than someone who could have taken different action."[74] Adding a final comment that demonstrates why one needs to be strong and resilient like water, Pfeiffer says, "My mission is to help other teens. I want to help anyone I can," she told *The Today Show*. "If I help one teen, I will feel—if I make one bully think twice before bullying, I would feel 100 percent better."[75]

Topic For Discussion   It's natural to feel angry or outraged when someone makes an Imposter Profile about you. So how do you behave better than your bully? In other words, how do you take the high road in order to hold your head up and maintain your pride? What are some effective, creative, and resilient ways to overcome after being a target of an Imposter Profile?

VOCAB WORDS

Criminal Impersonation: A person who impersonates or pretends to be another, and does an act, in such assumed character, with intent to obtain a benefit or to injure or defraud another.

Defame: To damage someone's reputation, character, or good name by slander or libel.

Retaliation: To pay back (an injury) in kind.

All I ask is one thing . . . and I'm asking this particularly of young people . . . please do not be cynical. For the record, it's my least favorite quality. It doesn't lead anywhere. Nobody in life gets exactly what they thought they were going to get. But if you work really hard and you're kind, amazing things will happen. I'm telling you. Amazing things will happen. I'm telling you. It's just true.
—Conan O'Brien

Imposter Profile Handouts
Combat: Group Activity
Threat Level Assessment

Low-Risk

An Imposter Profile about you shows up and the statements about you are mildly annoying and/or embarrassing (but not cruel or excessive). It shows no photos of you and no identifying information other than your name. What do you do?

_____

_____

_____

_____

_____

_____

_____

_____

Guarded Risk

The Imposter Profile shows up about you. You've already tried to get it shut it down and/or told a parent or teacher. The website still hasn't been taken down after a week and lots of people are starting to add to it or comment on it. What do you do?

_____

_____

_____

_____

_____

_____

_____

_____

Elevated Risk

The Imposter Profile shares personal information about you that threatens your reputation or repeatedly harasses you with very embarrassing information (whether or not the information is true) or posts obscene statements or lists your personal info (email address, cell phone number, address, where to find you alone, etc.) What do you do?

_____

_____

_____

_____

_____

_____

_____

High-Risk

The bully behind the Imposter Profile gets a lot of people to post nasty comments about you or "hate speech" comments (any words targeting your race, gender, disability, or sexual orientation) or says on the site that they are going to stalk and harass or kill you or tells you to kill yourself. What do you do?

_____

_____

_____

_____

_____

_____

four

Internet Tactics: Haters' Club

Haters' Club:

Haters have a special link to one another and they tend to fuel each other's hate by hating in groups. —Urban Dictionary

With this tactic, a mob is involved in bullying the target, often prompted by discriminatory aspects like race, gender, or sexual orientation. The bullies start up a website or social networking profile with the target's image and denigrating information so that followers can persistently defame the target's reputation with name-calling, misinformation, lies, and other forms of harassment.

Getting Started

Lesson Rundown   Students are introduced to the concept of a Haters' Club, which translates the concept of herd mentality to websites, social networking profiles, or message boards to denigrate and persecute an individual.

Objective   Students will be able to:

- understand the stages that lead to a systematic persecution of an individual;
- make individual choices within the group behavior of "herd mentality";
- assess how to defend themselves ethically and legally in escalating situations;
- resist revenge and draw upon inner strength and "self-talk" to build one's self-image back up again.

Time Needed   The Understand, Combat, and Transform sections are structured to be conducted within a typical classroom requiring 30-40 minutes of lesson time. The Prevent sections may require 30-60 minutes as they go more in-depth and may prompt more conversation. Total estimated time for the Haters' Club Unit is 2–3 hours, and will vary in an after-school or workshop environment.

Teacher Prep   Review any group or individual activities ahead of time for materials needed to maximize in-class time.

Equipment/
Supplies Needed   Computers with Internet access can be used for high-tech activities. Otherwise, paper and writing materials can be used for low-tech activities.

Vocab Words   Defined at the end of this section.

Handouts   *Group Activity I: 8 Stages of Genocide; Individual Activity: The 5 C's; Group Activity II: The 5 C's; The Line Game, Threat Level Assessments.*

For The Educator

Tactic Overview

This chapter explains how a Haters' Club starts, why it' s created, who participates, and ways to help students avoid this type of tactic. Because this chapter deals with a more complicated set of **herd mentality** behaviors, it is probably more of an appropriate lesson for students entering into or already in high school. In this chapter, students will learn how to make ethical choices around the participation in a Haters' Club and what to do if they have been a target of one.

How A Haters' Club Happens: In this tactic, the "bully" is made up of multiple perpetrators who all know each other and form a group identity to harass the target. A Haters' Club is usually started by one or two bullies relying on the viral participation of their followers to post negative and derogatory statements about the target. This tactic is also known as "**trolling**" and if you ever want an in-depth definition of what motivates individuals or gangs to completely demoralize their target, check out "Dealing With Trolls" in our Resources section online.

Though a Haters' Club uses the same technological tools as an Imposter Profile, no impersonation of the target is required. It is very similar to the tactic of a Digital Pile On—only much more extreme. The purpose is not merely to make fun of an individual—it's pure vitriol aimed at the target to make him or her feel hated by everyone. The anonymous bullies easily set up an account on a social networking site or a private online forum. Usually the whole thing starts with a posted rumor or defamatory language about the target. Often, they scour the Internet for anything the target has willingly revealed online for fodder. The Haters' Club gathers steam with each follower who joins and/or posts comments. It can become very powerful very quickly depending on how many multiple bystanders visit the site. Those bystanders who **lurk** can get caught up in the drama and turn into followers by posting something negative. Often, when the drama can't be heightened by finding any real dirt on the target, the bullies will construct **logical fallacies** to provide "support" for their false conclusions. Anonymous followers can also be **trolls** and trolls can additionally set up false identities called **sock puppets**. If the target's defenders and allies learn of the Haters' Club, they will attempt to post positive comments or attack the attackers on the site itself. Either way, each new post gives the Haters' Club more negative energy and more visibility—and that plays right into the motive of the bullies who feed off the attention.

Bullies who start a Haters' Club are much like any other hate group that uses **propaganda**, lies, **rumor-mongering**, and **defamation** to harm individuals and groups they target, while using intimidation to silence potential allies of the target. The supporters of the Holocaust employed eight specific tactics very similar, psychologically, to a Haters' Club, which we will discuss in this chapter. Because of the power it quickly generates, a Haters' Club must be taken down and dealt with immediately. The following scenario was inspired by a real-life Haters' Club that put a high school girl at the brink of suicide, before, thankfully, an entire community of strangers reversed much of the damage by flooding the girl with letters of support, love, and compassion.

VOCAB WORDS

Defamation: Act of injuring another's reputation by any slanderous communication, written or oral.

Herd Mentality: A fear-based reaction to peer pressure which makes individuals behave all alike to avoid feeling "left behind" from the group.

Logical Fallacies: A collapse in logic often used in debate to mislead or distract people from the real issue.

Lurk: To read but not contribute to the discussion in a newsgroup, chat room, or other online forum.

Propaganda: Information, ideas, or rumors deliberately spread widely to help or harm a person, group, movement, institution, nation, etc.

Rumor-mongering: To engage in the spreading of rumors.

Sock Puppet: The act of creating a fake online identity to praise, defend, or construct the illusion of support for one's self, allies, or company.

Troll/Trolling: Someone who posts negative messages in an online community to provoke other users to react.

Scenario
Anna's Story

Print the below story and hand out to the students. For more interactivity, assign someone to read it to the entire class.

Torn Down and Built Back Up

A headache and stomachache were the first warning. Fourteen-year-old Anna sat in home-room class, stiff with fear, knowing what was about to happen. She had been diagnosed with epilepsy when she was a baby and had conquered years of daily medications and multiple surgeries. Her parents had always homeschooled her, as they worried about her seizures, but this year, Anna just wanted to be a regular high school freshman like everybody else.

She'd been feeling great for months, but now the symptoms were all-too-familiar—she could feel it coming on. Just after the bell rang in homeroom, the worst had begun. Anna felt herself slump over in her chair as she collapsed on the floor in an epileptic seizure. She had no sense of time, but it must have been minutes. When it was over, she lay on the floor, dazed, looking up at all the faces hovering over her. As the teacher helped her up and led her to the nurse's office, she noticed everyone around her staring. No one said anything.

The next day, some of the kids at school began to make fun of her and started gossiping about what could have caused the seizure. They started a rumor that it was because she was taking drugs. When she heard that, Anna started to cry. She hadn't been in a public high school for very long and didn't know how to fight back against the lies and meanness. She began having anxiety attacks and hid in bathroom stalls between classes, just so she didn't have to be seen or talk to anyone. Somehow, this made the kids meaner.

They took her new backpack later that week and dragged it through the mud. A few days after that, a girl named Kendra from her school started an "Anna Haters' Club" on a website with all kinds of nasty comments. Anna couldn't bear to look at it but she *had* to check it every day to see what they were saying about her. Then, certain kids at school began wearing "Die Anna" wristbands. At first it was just a few kids at school who were part of this mean game, but now it seemed everyone was out to get her. The anonymous mob behind Anna's Haters' Club wrote on the website that if she snitched to her mother or the school, they'd "break every bone in her body." Anna began to feel suicidal thoughts every single night. She couldn't tell her mother, too afraid that if her mother did something to try to stop it, it would only make it worse and they'd come after her even harder.

Her mother found out anyway when the mother of one of Anna's friends learned of what was happening. The principal tried to speak to the parents of all the kids who were part of the Haters' Club, but, because her school had no cyberbullying policy, nothing adults were doing seemed to help Anna's situation. Anna actually had to transfer schools not just once, *but twice* to escape the Haters' Club that seemed to follow her everywhere on the Internet. Yet that still didn't stop the cyberbullying from starting all over again every few months.

Anna was at her lowest point when her mother finally took drastic steps and informed the local newspaper about everything that had happened. When the story came out, two sisters from a nearby school, Sarah and Emily, began writing kind letters to Anna. Emily just wanted Anna to know there were at least two strangers on her side and that she wasn't alone. The sisters got their friends to write to Anna, too, and the kindness began to spread. More than 3,000 letters all over the world from little kids to grandparents poured in to support Anna, as they shared their own pain about being bullied. Anna had been on a dangerous and downward path to possibly ending her life, but was saved by the kindness of strangers. Today she is back to being homeschooled and has more balance and peace in her life.

Step I: Understand

Objective Students will be able to:
- identify with the systematic psychological process leading up to a Haters' Club;
- understand how bullies develop a group identity;
- avoid being a bystander or henchman to a Haters' Club.

Time Needed 55 minutes.

Teacher Prep Copy handouts of the Scenario for the class, or display through a wall projector and have students vocalize the roles of the characters.

Equipment/ Copier. Computers with Internet access
Supplies Needed (high-tech) or paper and pencils (low-tech).

Vocab Words Defined at the end of this section.

Overview

Start with the Topic for Discussion to get students warmed up. Gradually move on to show them the various roles people play in this particular tactic.

Establish Group See the guidelines in **Appendix C** in order to get the most out of
Guidelines your group discussions in class.

Topic for Discussion Ask your students what their definition of "**hater**" is. Do you think all of the kids in the Haters' Club started off as bullies? How many were bystanders who participated in the incident as a form of entertainment? Then ask them why it is so hard to stand up to a group of them. When everyone has had a chance to voice his or her observations, refer to below.

Define Tactic Define what a Haters' Club is. Ask them if they've ever seen or have been part of one and what they learned from it.

For The Student:
A Broader
Perspective

Online conflict isn't always clear-cut. Once you've gotten through the Topic For Discussion, ask your students to define the roles of each participant in the scenario. We've provided multiple perspectives below to help students gain insight.

From The Bully's Perspective: Kendra, the bully who started the initial Haters' Club, had always disliked Anna, though she never really understood why. When Anna had collapsed that day on the floor, Kendra couldn't get it out of her mind. She began to really feel disgust and loathing whenever she saw Anna in the hallway. Kendra invited a close group of friends to join her "Die Anna" website and it became their secret club. Kendra was delighted to see another friend had made them all "Die Anna" wristbands to wear at school. Kendra thoroughly enjoyed all this attention and underground popularity. Some people began to protest on Kendra's secret site, saying it was mean and they were going to tell if it didn't stop. But now that more people were following this club than before, Kendra wasn't about to let Anna or one of her dumb friends stop them. All she had to do was threaten Anna once. Soon, no one else was protesting their secret club. It grew and grew until other kids from other high schools were joining in on it, too. It was getting so big Kendra began to feel like a rock star. If she had that much power, she wondered how far she could go. She got online and started a new topic, typing: "How Many People Want To See Anna Kill Herself?" Kendra couldn't wait to see how many people would comment on this one.

Kendra personifies what Barbara Coloroso, author of *The Bully, The Bullied, and The Bystander,* calls, "arrogance in action." "Kids who bully have an air or superiority that is often a mask to cover up deep hurt and a feeling of inadequacy," writes Coloroso. "They rationalize that their supposed superiority entitles them to hurt someone they hold in contempt, when, in reality, it is an excuse to put someone down so they can feel 'up'. "[76]

From The Target's Perspective: After Anna's seizure, she knew kids were making fun of her at school, but she had no idea it had moved online until a friend told her about the "Die Anna" website. When she found it, she couldn't believe what she was seeing. Why did so many people put their energy into this? Did they really hate her so much that they could say these things and not care how it made her feel? One of her friends posted something on the site to defend her, but it didn't make Anna feel very protected. At first, Anna waited to see if it would go away, terrified that if she told her mom, Kendra and her friends would find other ways to make her life even worse. Anna was a shy girl who caused no trouble in school. She was confused about their reasons for going after her. The fact that there were so many people joining in scared her. She began to really wonder: if everybody hated her so much, maybe there was something truly hateful about her, otherwise why would so many people join in and do this to her? As the cyberbullying grew, she became increasingly powerless, afraid to fight for herself, afraid to tell. Her stomachaches and headaches appeared frequently, and she was terrified of having another seizure at school. She began to find as many excuses she could not to go. She had many dark and anguished thoughts about killing herself in the weeks that followed—exactly what the bullies were pushing for her to do. In a way, Anna was relieved when her friend's mother had finally told Anna's mother what had been happening.

The police couldn't help them; changing schools didn't help. Only when her story came out in the local newspaper did Anna felt that things might turn around. Thousands of strangers wrote her letters, telling her that she was a good person, that she wasn't alone, and that the Haters' Club was not to be trusted or believed. Thanks to those two kind sisters and all of these strangers who wrote her personal letters, Anna began to believe once again that the world wasn't out to "get" her—that what had happened to her was the result of an immature group of bullies whose tactics were fueled by the power of their numbers.

From The Bystanders' Perspective: All bullies need is an audience. There were hundreds of bystanders who **lurked** on the "Die Anna" Haters' Club website for entertainment to see what would be posted every day. It was like a reality show, fascinating to some, but to others a horrible thing they couldn't stop looking at. Despite their various feelings on the subject, everyone who commented on the "Die Anna" website played right into the bullies' plan. The bigger it got, the more the Haters' Club spread like wildfire. Of course, the kids at Anna's school who viewed the website probably didn't see themselves as **accomplices** to the bully, but when one chooses not to take an active role in defending the target, one actually *supports* the bully by default.

From The Followers' Perspective: At first, one or two bullies were Anna's tormentors. But as the popularity of the Haters' Club grew online, passive bystanders became active followers simply by adding a comment here or there. In this case, Anna's Haters' Club gave all members of this group a **shared group identity**—something that bonded them and made them feel superior to her. When teens tend to get in groups with a negative purpose, individual ideas and morals get swayed by the group's mindset, which is not only dangerous, it almost always results in doing something that is morally wrong.

From The Allies' Perspective: In the first few weeks after the Haters' Club showed up, a few people who had stuck up for Anna online and in school got threatened. As terrible as her allies felt for Anna, no one wanted to be the next target. They were too scared to tell an adult because there was no cyberbullying policy in their school. They didn't think one or two kids would be able to stop it by themselves and they had no confidence that adults would be able to either. Finally, one of Anna's friends couldn't stand to see what was happening. She knew everything they were doing to Anna was wrong; and facing her own fears about what would happen to her, she first told her parents, who then told Anna's mother. In the end, this brave ally's actions caused a chain reaction to lift Anna away from a dangerous choice she was considering and helped her get to a better place.

> **In the end, we will remember not the words of our enemies,**
> **but the silence of our friends.**
> **—Martin Luther King Jr.**

Group Activity Overview

The Eight Stages Of Genocide created by Gregory H. Stanton, President, Genocide Watch, are: *classification, symbolization, dehumanization, organization, polarization, identification, extermination,* and *denial.* See the definitions and the handout at the end of this chapter for further detail.[77] Though the material in The Eight Stages of Genocide handout covers disturbing topics, use it as a comparative tool for understanding this tactic. Note: the language in these stages is pretty sophisticated for a teen audience and will likely need some paraphrasing. When people do not know on which side of the moral fence they will choose to stand (i.e. defending an innocent target versus passively observing the systematic and psychological breakdown of that person), what you have is the germination of these Eight Stages. Even a basic understanding of these concepts at an early age will help prepare students to make ethical decisions later on in life about more complex issues.

Group Activity   Break your students into eight small groups and assign each group a stage in "The Eight Stages of Genocide" handout at the end of this chapter. Ask each small group to list how a modern day Haters' Club is very similar to the stage they are assigned and have someone in their group write it down. Ask students to answer to this question: "If we were to do the right thing at this stage, we would . . ." Each group can now present their examples and their answers to the class.

Teacher	A made-for-TV movie, *Odd Girl Out (2005)*, is the story of a girl who
Takeaway Tip	is on the receiving end of rumors, extreme relational bullying, and
	an online Haters' Club. If you have time, rent this film and skim
	through relevant parts, including how it affects the main character,
	to give your class a visual experience of this tactic.

VOCAB WORDS

Accomplice: A person who joins with another in carrying out some plan (especially an unethical or illegal plan).

Hater: A person who simply cannot be happy for another person's success. Instead, he or she makes a point of exposing a flaw in that person.

Lurk: To read but not contribute to the discussion in a newsgroup, chat room, or other online forum.

Shared Group Identity: The shared social characteristics, such as worldview, language, values, and ideological system, that evolve from membership in an ethnic group.

Step II: Prevent

Objective Students will be able to:

- understand what kinds of behaviors contribute to group affiliation;
- appreciate, rather than instigate, conflict over everyone's differences;
- protect themselves with behavioral and technological strategies to prevent being the target of a Haters' Club.

Time Needed 30-60 minutes.

Teacher Prep Read any passage ahead of class time labeled "For the Educator." You will need pieces of blank paper for each student. A printer is needed to print out transcripts. The alternate group activity simply requires students to physically stand up.

Equipment/ Supplies Needed A computer lab and printer would be beneficial for this section, but the individual and group activity can both be done in low-tech classrooms with paper and pencils.

Vocab Words Defined at the end of this section.

> **"Take sides. Neutrality helps the oppressor, never the victim. Silence encourages the tormentor, never the tormented."**
> **—Elie Wiesel**

For The Educator: Conflict Resolution Concepts

In middle and high school, certain students seem to always get singled out and persecuted for being "different." The power base, therefore, lies with those who are all perceived as "the same." The conflict resolution point for this particular tactic is to get the students to appreciate, rather than view with suspicion, the **diversity** between and among individuals and groups. The goal is to understand how **group affiliation** can be used both the right way—and the wrong way. According to authors Richard J. Bodine, Donna K. Crawford, and Fred Schrumpf, the authors of *Creating the Peaceable School: A Comprehensive Program for Teaching Conflict Resolution*: "When differences are acknowledged and appreciated and when the conflicting parties build on one another's strengths—a climate is created that nurtures the self-worth of each individual and provides opportunities for fulfillment to each."[78]

For a practical in-class activity around group affiliation, we turn to the work of Patti DeRosa, President of Changeworks Consulting, and Ulric Johnson, Assistant Dean, School of Human Services at Springfield College. Together, they created The 5 C's, which are five categories to help us define who we are and who we identify with.[79] Be sure to go over these definitions with your students because they will be used in both our Individual and Group Activity.

The 5 C's

- **Color**: These characteristics you're born with and usually can't change.
- **Culture**: These are characteristics of the group with which you identify.
- **Clout**: This is the amount of power, status, and influence you have.
- **Character**: These are characteristics that represent your personality traits.
- **Context**: This determines where, when, and who you live with.

Students will naturally look for differences when examining the above five categories. So, this exercise needs to refocus that perspective. As William J. Kreidler, author of *Conflict in the Middle School* states, "Research tells us that if we want students to appreciate people different from themselves, they are more likely to do this if they are in an environment that generally appreciates diversity."[80] Therefore, with our Individual Activity, we will be looking for positive connections among the students, using the above five categories.

Individual Activity   Refer to the handout at the end of this chapter for the Individual Activity. Ask students to review the five categories in the 5 C's handout and spend some time writing a word or a sentence that describes themselves in each of the five categories.

Self-Defense On the board, write down two columns: **Behavior** and **Tech Defense**. Ask your class to volunteer their own suggestions to prevent being the target of a Haters' Club and follow up by presenting the strategies below.

Behavior

As mentioned in other chapters, anyone who is perceived as "different" in any minor way is vulnerable to being a bully's target. You can't and shouldn't have to change who you are just to avoid being mistreated, but there are specific behavioral changes you can make to prevent social missteps. The key is to develop a keen awareness about the social structure of people at your school.

- **Zip The Lip On The Deets**: Unfair as it is, girls still endure the double standard and **public shaming** over their romantic/sexual lives. Girls, you need to be extremely careful about sharing these kinds of details with anyone, including those you trust. In this case, secrets equal power. As for boys, spreading rumors and gossip just makes you look untrustworthy and needy for attention. Trusting best friends with this kind of confidential information often has a way of backfiring, and many cyberbullying incidents simply start because someone used that information against the target by attacking his or her reputation.

- **Know Who Holds The Power**: In general, it is smart to be aware of who runs the powerful cliques in your school and observe how they treat others. So many offline conflicts start because a girl starts dating the "ex" of another girl who is part of a powerful clique, or a guy has an aggressive moment or is boasting about another guy without realizing how many of the other guy's buddies will back him up. Be aware of the people in your school who cause drama, take offense at every little thing and like to start trouble. . .and stay far away from them.

- **Address Conflict/Rumors in Person**: If a rumor starts swirling about you or you make a mistake with someone, never go online and deal with it there. As calmly as possible, tell your friends and acquaintances the truth and let them be your **advocate**. Or, if you need to apologize, do so *in person*. If the conflict starts in the "real world" with a bully, you need to make it known in a confident way that you will not tolerate being targeted or picked on. If you're shy and need an adult to help you prepare what to say, get that help right away.

- **Individual vs. Gang**: When cyberbullying is one-on-one, depending on the severity of the situation, you might be able to handle it yourself. But the moment it becomes a **gang of bullies**, immediately tell an adult—no matter what the bullies say to threaten you. If you can't go to your parent, go to a teacher, counselor, or mentor to help you plan a strategy. Do not assume "it will die down" when a group is involved. It always gets worse. School authorities will take quicker action when a group or gang of bullies is involved.

- **Monitor All Online Profiles**: This is the time to track down any information you've left online about yourself and to shut down any "forgotten" social networking profile you never use anymore. (Use the "Super Logoff" Technique in the Prevention section of Imposter Profile chapter.) Scour the information out there for anything that can be used against you. In severe situations, it is best to disable all online accounts, take down anything you don't want to be seen, and be very cautious about what you choose to put out on the 'Net about yourself.

- **Stick Close To Friends**: This is a time when your friends need to have your back, because there is safety in numbers. Find somebody at school (an older student) who people respect and ask that person to help you and be your **advocate**, but do not use your friends to fight this battle for you. Multiple people involved in a conflict can instead escalate the situation and weaken your position legally.

- **School Mediation**: As soon as a gang of bullies has been identified, record as many details as you can remember and give it to your teacher or school authority to put into a **Scene Survey** (**Appendix B**). Identify who are the true bullies and who the followers/henchmen are. The school may be able to help by bringing in a professional **mediator** to help you talk to the people you are having conflict with and resolve it so that the cyberbullying stops.

Tech Defense

In a computer lab, these exercises can be easily done in a class period, depending on the amount of time everyone has. This is an excellent exercise to help students get familiar with how technology can aid them before they ever experience cyberbullying.

- **Monitor Online Reputation**: Create a **Google Alert** with your real name and any nicknames you're known by. Google Alerts are email updates of the latest relevant Google results (web, news, etc.) based on a choice of query or topic.[81] So if someone has posted something about you, an email will come to your inbox and you will be the first to know. Use a free reputation monitor service that scours the Internet for all photos, blogs, forums, videos, and social media that reference back to your name such as Social Mention (www.socialmention.com).

- **Reputation Management:** Reputation.com (www.reputation.com) and Reputation Armor (www.reputationarmor.com) are two of the most recommended online reputation managers. Some of these services can destroy certain online listings; other strategies can push negative content down on search engines. See our Resources for more recommendations. If you've been cyberbullied, it is absolutely worth it for you to schedule a free consultation along with your parents and explain the circumstances to an expert who deals with this kind of cyberbullying situation all of the time.

- **Tell An Anonymous Tip Line:** SchoolTipline (www.schooltipline.com) and Speak Out Hotline (www.speakouthotline.org) are online tools that can be used through the Internet and cell phones to instantly provide anonymous feedback and information-sharing in school communities. SchoolTipline allows you and your classmates to send and receive instant information on bullying to school administration and staff. The way the service is set up, bogus tips are instantly filtered out from genuine tips, allowing bystanders, in particular, more control in helping a target without putting their own reputations at risk.

Group Activity   Refer to the 5 C's handout at the end of this chapter for the Group Activity. Now that students have the 5 C's categories filled out about themselves from the Individual Activity, ask them to pair up with a partner and compare their characteristics to one another. (Try to not let friends pair up with one another.) In the blank box below, list as many of the same shared characteristics that each student has to one another.

Alternative Group Activity: The Line Game can be used in conjunction with the 5 C's or used on its own. See end of the chapter for more details.

VOCAB WORDS

Advocate: One who pleads on another's behalf or "sticks up for" the rights of someone else.

Diversity: Understanding that each individual is unique, and recognizing our individual differences.

Gang of Bullies: Multiple bullies with a group affiliation who attack one person.

Group Affiliation: To associate oneself as a member of a larger group that shares the same characteristics.

Mediator: A negotiator who helps solve the differences between two people in conflict.

Public Shaming: To cause someone to feel shame, a strong sense of guilt, embarrassment, unworthiness, or disgrace in public as a form of punishment.

Scene Survey: A rational "shorthand" system to get all the facts about a cyberbullying incident before making a plan or decision. This can be found in **Appendix B**.

Step III: Combat

Objective

Students will be able to:

- identify low- to high-risk online situations;
- assess possible solutions to remedy conflict;
- practice making thoughtful, deliberate choices on how to react to the threat.

Time Needed

30 minutes.

Teacher Prep

Read any section ahead of class time labeled "For the Educator." Make a copy each of the Threat Level Assessments to hand out to four small groups.

Equipment/ Supplies Needed

Copier for handouts and pencils for students.

Vocab Words

Defined at the end of this section.

In the following section we use our own version of the US Department of Defense's concept of "Threat Levels" when providing students action steps to take.

Note: the advice in this section does not purport to be legal advice. We have consulted with cyberbullying experts to help parents, educators, and students know what to do in a Haters' Club situation.

Immediate Steps To Take

Because this particular tactic almost always has multiple perpetrators, a student needs to tell a parent or the school authorities immediately. It now puts the responsibility upon the parent, the school, and possibly the school's attorney to put a stop to the bullies' behavior. This is the kind of tactic that makes having a clear, school-wide cyberbullying policy necessary, for if it goes on too long unchecked it may invariably lead to student harm, criminal charges, and lawsuits. We also recommend making an appointment with a Reputation Manager consultant to discuss what one can do to control the negative information appearing under one's name online.

Website Penalties: The Haters' Club website may be breaking the rules of the hosting website or service if the perpetrator registers the site under the student's real name. Let the Webmaster of the site know immediately or get a trusted adult to help you.

Reporting Abuse: In most social networking profiles, there is a link at the bottom of every thread to report abuse. A parent or school authority needs to be informed right away. The next action sends the bully a message stating that they are aware of the Haters' Club and that it will not be tolerated on or offline or further action will be taken. A **Scene Survey** (**Appendix B**) needs to be filled out so that all parties can be identified. If your school has an **IT professional**, bring that person in to try to track the **ISP** of the Haters' Club profile and uncover as many of the identities of the anonymous bullies who have contributed to it as you can.

Threat Level Assessment

In this section, the group activity comes before the lesson. This allows students to "pre-play" how they might react to each escalating situation. *Educators will need to make copies of the four Threat Level Assessments at the end of this chapter before the group activity can begin.*

Group Activity   Split the class into four small groups and ask them to retreat to each corner of the room. Assign each group a hypothetical situation ranging from Low-Risk to High-Risk (handouts found at the end of this chapter). Appoint a group leader to read the Threat Level Assessment on each handout to the group, and give each group a chance to write down their solutions to each hypothetical situation. After each group is done, ask the group leader (starting with Low Risk) to read the group's suggestions out loud to the class. Educators can provide the correct answer from the "What To Do" guide below for each Threat Level.

1. **Low-Risk**: The Haters' Club website or social networking profile shows up with a few mild insults posted about you. It looks like an amateur job that was done without much thought. It doesn't show any photos of you or identifying information other than your name.

   Frequency: It is not taken seriously; receives a low number of comments.

   What To Do: A parent or school authority should still be informed so the adults can effectively intervene and help the student get it taken down. Report the site to the Webmaster immediately. Even if the language online is protected as "freedom of speech," it is still a tactic used to defame and harass an individual, and that is against the terms of service of most every reputable website or social networking company. The next action is to have the parent and/or school authorities instruct the bullies (and their parents if necessary) to delete the Haters' Club account. Inform the bullies that if the Haters' Club is ever reinstated or reconfigured under a different name and uploaded anywhere else on the Internet, further disciplinary action will be taken.

2. **Guarded Risk**: The Haters' Club website or social networking profile displays your name, your face, and is using information you posted about yourself against you in every mean and nasty way possible. It is still up after twenty-four hours of reporting it and nothing has changed. More negative anonymous comments are added daily.

Frequency: Posts/comments are increasing by the day and you are starting to get real-life (offline) bullying because of it.

What To Do: Follow all the steps in Low-Risk first. Do a **Scene Survey** (**Appendix B**). Try to pinpoint the identity of the alleged bully if you don't know who is actually behind it. Are there certain words or phrases on the site or profile that are used by people who you know? Ask an advocate to create an anonymous **alias** to gain access to the Haters' Club profile or any closed social networks the bullies belong to. This should be for information and evidence gathering only and not as a form of reverse cyberbullying. Use a screen capture program like Cyberbully Alert to instantly preserve evidence (www.cyberbullyalert.com) and print it out as soon as possible or send it to someone who can print it out for you. Do this quickly because most evidence "disappears" once the bullies know you're onto them. If you need help, ask the school's IT professional to address and preserve evidence or hire someone to do this

Technically, if any of the students who are part of the Haters' Club have posted comments on school property or during school class times, they are liable for disciplinary action. But even if they've posted from home, they may still be under the school's jurisdiction, particularly if it can be proven that off-campus bullying is having negative consequences at school. Depending on the nature of the content posted, you should be working with his or her parents and the school to determine at what point the police should be involved.

3. **Elevated Risk**: The Haters' Club website or social networking profile goes full-force, with multiple people joining as a gang of bullies. The bullies use tactics like **flaming**, harassment, rumors, and ridicule. Their language is abusive, profane, or posts your personal info (email address, phone number) to encourage more abuse.

    What To Do: Contact the police in order to **subpoena** the website adminis-trator to determine who started the Haters' Club and any **IP addresses** of those who have participated. Work with the authorities to identify the anonymous perpetrators. Continue to save and print any evidence of the abuse as it happens. You and your parents should be working with the school administrators at this point, informing them when anything new happens and providing them with evidence. By now, the school administrators should be dealing directly with the bullies and their parents.

Ask school administrators if they will put an official message out to the originators of the Haters' Club website or profile (if it has still not been removed) that any further harassment or any other new website will be tracked, preserved, and turned over to the police. The fact that many participants are "piling on" at this point makes it much more likely that the bullying is having a big impact at school. Encourage all students to participate in an anonymous Tip Line. Most likely there will still be some bullying backlash online (because it spoils their fun), but it sends a clear message to them that they are no longer unaccountable and anonymous.

4. **High-Risk**: The bullies are posting lewd and/or severely derogatory statements about you or threatening you and encouraging others to do the same. Or someone posts "**hate speech**" (any words that disrespect your race, gender, disability, sexual orientation) or makes statements to provoke other unknown people to stalk and harass you or posts threatening comments suggesting you will be hurt or killed.

Frequency: Even if this happens once, it is considered high-risk.

What To Do: You should follow every single one of the "Threat Level" steps leading up to this one. Contact the police with all of your saved evidence. Once online tactics turn into full-on cyber-harassment or threats of safety, the more help the student and his or her parents will get from law enforcement to determine if the bully is breaking the law. Ask for a consultation with an attorney whose expertise is in cyberbullying or defamation to see whether the written abuse may be prosecutable. The school authorities should by now have had conversations with all of the bullies and bystanders and their parents that if they continue to harass you, they may be subject to legal action. Even if your parents aren't prepared to make this a case at this point, the bullies, the bystanders, and their parents need to understand the full extent of consequences. Because ugly and untrue statements may still be linked to the student's name in search engines, we recommend talking to a reputation management service for advice. Initial consultations are usually free.

One last word on this subject (and this is a personal opinion), we've studied cases where the harassment was so prevalent in schools that operated without a cyber-bullying policy, the parents were without a clue, and even police were ineffective in stopping it. If the cyberbullying gets to this point and begins to compromise the student's mental health and sense of safety—get the student out of there. Temporarily home school the student or move him or her to a different school system altogether. While some might argue that doing so "only lets the bullies win," we see no good that comes from forcing a student to be terrorized every day in a toxic school environment. The priority is to help the student lessen his or her anxieties in order to heal from and transform the experience in a safer environment.

Topic For Discussion   Now that everyone has had a chance to see all the hypothetical Threat Levels in this chapter, ask your students where they draw the line. At what point would they be motivated to intervene on a friend's behalf as an ally? How about a bullied classmate who wasn't necessarily a friend?

VOCAB WORDS

Alias: A false name used to conceal one's identity.

Flaming: Online "fights" using electronic messages with angry and/or vulgar language.

Hate Speech: Speech not protected by the First Amendment, because it is intended to foster hatred against individuals or groups based on race, religion, gender, sexual preference, place of national origin, or other improper classification.

IP Address: This is each computer's numerical label for host or network interface identification and location addressing. This can be pinpointed to identify the bully's computer.

ISP Provider: An ISP (Internet Service Provider) is a company that collects a monthly or yearly fee in exchange for providing the subscriber with Internet access.

IT Professional: An employee of the school who manages and administers the school's entire Information Technology systems.

Subpoena: A legal document that commands the recipient to produce evidence necessary to the resolution of a legal matter or controversy.

Step IV: Transform

Objective   Students will be able to:

- empathize with those who have been attacked by putting themselves in the target's shoes;
- practice making thoughtful, deliberate choices on how to react after the threat;
- "pre-play" how they would deal with being targets of a Haters' Club if it happened again to them.

Time Needed   30 minutes.

Teacher Prep   Allow students to read this section by themselves. For younger students, translate the concepts for better understanding.

Equipment/   Paper and pencils for students to take notes during Topic for Discussion.
Supplies Needed

Teacher Tip   This section is best absorbed if read first by the educator and used as a basis for a Topic For Discussion at the end.

Note: The Transform section is meant for the students to read on their own, as this is our advice to them directly. Present this as an in-class reading or a take-home reading assignment, and then come back as a class and introduce the Topic For Discussion. For younger students, educators might want to translate some of these concepts.

For The Student: The Damage Is Done, How To Cope

Chuck Nguyen, our martial artist/bullying expert for this section, has this to say about a Haters' Club:

There is nothing more damaging and **disempowering** for a young person than feeling alone and alienated. If you walk into a cafeteria on any day in a typical high school, what you see are groups of students eating together. It's not the food that binds them together—it's the social interaction. Rarely do you see a student sitting alone in a high school cafeteria; that is not the social norm. And while the cafeteria is where lots of positive social interaction happens, at the same time, much harm can equally happen in the form of social alienation and a hateful **herd mentality** toward single individuals.

Being a target of a Haters' Club on the Internet is a similar experience to being socially targeted and isolated in a school's cafeteria. You will feel vulnerable, lonely, and disempowered. The bullies have tactically used their power and popularity to weaken you and purposely take all opportunity for connection, friendship, and support away.

How do you transform this experience? First, tell people what has happened. Do not keep it inside and do not think you have to deal with this alone. To heal and rebuild yourself, it is necessary to gather additional support from positive adults or friends. Many people who have been hurt in life are unable to move away emotionally from the experience. Don't be one of them—*stuck forever in an experience you didn't ask for.* To be stuck emotionally can be as damaging as experiencing the physical or verbal abuse over and over. This is the time to be your own best friend and make a determined plan to move on. Once you are feeling safer and ready to face bullies again, it is time to prepare mentally. The idea of **resiliency** is important here, and here's how to do it:

Build Your Strength, One Sentence at a Time

Whether you begin your list on paper or in your head as "self-talk"—this is the time to take stock of what is good and valuable about yourself so you can build on your strength and move on from the aftermath of what happened. On the left side of the paper, write the words "I am" and on the right side write, "I am not." Under the "I am" list, write down phrases about you that are true. For example: "I am worth something, loved by my family, respected by my friends, etc." Under the "I am not" list, also assess what is true. For example, "I am not what they think I am. I am not hated by the entire world, or stupid, a bad person" (or any of the

111

other false statements they've assigned to you).

Now, examine the "I am not" list carefully to check off what item or misconception is defined by the bullies and what either feels "true" or "not true" to yourself. This process is a step toward personal growth and increasing the your self-confidence. To examine our weaknesses is also an essential step in becoming stronger. The point of this exercise is to cultivate the kind of resiliency one needs to face adversity and injustice, especially when it is done in such an unfair, hateful, and cruel way.

Don't Give In . . . Or Up

To some degree, all of us have been targets of unfair judgment and hateful behavior in our lifetimes. We cannot control what others say and do to us, but we have a key to freedom in how we allow their judgments to affect us. We give our personal power away to the bullies when we become afraid of their disapproval and **derision**. On the other hand, we take personal power away from ourselves when we seek their acceptance. It takes practice to stop seeking someone's approval and/or reacting to their disapproval and derision. When you stop caring about either—the power they hold over you is gone. Hold onto your personal power; never give in to what the bullies believe is "true." Just because they are big in numbers, their collective opinion *is not a measure of truth.* There will always be groups of people who band together using their negative energies to make up lies where there are none, start personal attacks when the truth gets in the way of their agendas, and be mean and spiteful as a form of entertainment. You can never reason with these people; don't even try. Take the high road and try to live your life with dignity and balance. Those who know you well will always know your true value.

Resist Revenge

The second source of our sense of resiliency comes from not giving in to our human tendency to "fight fire with fire and hate with hate." It is tempting to want to "get back" at the bullies, but if you are vengeful and seeking to equal the score, you will only end up hurting your **integrity**. Furthermore, it will increase the bullying retaliation and ruin your chance of getting the school and the law to serve the bullies justice. View yourself as a person of enlightened dignity—and you will always rise above the people who choose to live their lives in darkness and ignorance. Not giving in to hate and revenge does not mean you have to be helpless.

Adult Intervention

Many adults cannot understand the cruelty of these tactics, nor can they always appreciate the subtlety that is needed to handle an online attack. It is not like traditional bullying because the stakes are much higher and some adults will give unhelpful advice such as, "Just ignore it," or, "Just fight them back." Do not listen to any adult who doesn't "get it." Continue to seek out adults who do, who can fully understand the situation, and who are willing to intervene for you. Do not get discouraged if you get bad or unhelpful advice—just keep searching for the right person to help you. Your anxiety will lesson when you have a strategy in place backed by adults who have more power than the bully. Ask what you can do to seek lawful justice. Every cyberbullying situation is different, so work on a strategy that helps you regain your personal power again.

Turn Your Pain Into Power

There are many targets who refuse to be silenced by the experience. They turn their anger, rage, and hurt into social outrage and eventually social activism. In 2011, a thirteen-year-old Connecticut eighth grade student named Alye Pollack took an "outside the box" approach to fighting her bullies with a legal and very effective counter tactic. She posted a video of herself on YouTube titled: "Words are worse than Sticks and Stones" in which she silently held up a series of signs that read: "I am bullied. Not a day has gone by without one of these words." The next signs she held up read: "freak," "ugly," and "weird." After that, she held up this sign: "I'm in therepy (sic) guidance more than my classes." She continued to hold up another sign: "I don't cut but I'm close." Finally she put up a sign that said: "Think before you say things . . . it might save lives."[82]

Because of this girl's silent but powerful video, more than a half million people have viewed it (at the time of this printing) and it has changed the power dynamic of the bullies. Her school's superintendent, under the spotlight of the news media, took steps to stop the bullying as thousands of strangers have pledged their comments to support her.[83] Her video has inspired multiple students to post their own anti-bullying videos. And her YouTube channel, Facebook page, and Twitter accounts now serve as a powerful anti-bullying message to all teens.

Students who have been targeted by a Haters' Club and group attacks can join a Civil Rights group in their school, or use the experience as an opportunity to start a support group for students who have had similar experiences. For example, a UK-based organization, Cyber-Mentors (cybermentors.org.uk) trains eighteen-to-twenty-five-year-olds to help younger students who've been cyberbullied how to cope. Each school in America should have a version of this, and if they don't, this would be a meaningful project to start in your school. Retelling one's story gives administrators, teachers, students, and the community a greater awareness of how deeply the wounds of cyberbullying go. Sometimes it takes time and slow efforts to bring awareness to this kind of tactic, and the only positive action is patient assessment, healing, and corrective action that is emotionally balanced.

To be resilient, **empowered**, and hopeful after being targeted by hate is the ultimate state of being. It is one of our most important human resources and abilities. The great leaders of our time have shown us the power of nonviolent reaction while not giving in to fear and hate. Mahatma Gandhi, Dr. Martin Luther King Jr., Nelson Mandela, and the Dali Lama are all great examples of people who have been targeted by a worldwide Haters' Club. These great leaders have achieved profound peace for their people by not giving in when they were hated, jailed, or faced with injustice. You have had an awful experience, but to transform it, examine how what you learned can be used for good to save other kids from experiencing the same thing.

Topic For Discussion   Ask your students: What is your school culture like in terms of how everyone responds to bullied kids? Is it helpful? Harmful? Indifferent? If your class were to start their own CyberMentors school project, who could they help and how?

VOCAB WORDS

Derision: A state of being laughed at or ridiculed.

Disempowered: You take away one's power, authority, or influence.

Empowered: To invest oneself with power.

Herd Mentality: A fear-based reaction to peer pressure which makes individuals behave all alike in order to avoid feeling "left behind" from the group.

Integrity: Adherence to moral and ethical principles; soundness of moral character; honesty.

Resiliency: The power or ability to recover readily from illness, depression, or adversity.

Haters' Club Handouts

This is the original text of this document and could not be altered for this workbook; however, it will likely need to be paraphrased for your students as some of the concepts and terms are complex.

Understand: Group Activity
The Eight Stages of Genocide

Genocide is a process that develops in eight stages that are predictable but not inexorable. At each stage, preventive measures can stop it. The process is not linear. Logically, later stages must be preceded by earlier stages. But all stages continue to operate throughout the process.

1. **CLASSIFICATION**: All cultures have categories to distinguish people into "us and them" by ethnicity, race, religion, or nationality: German and Jew, Hutu and Tutsi. Bipolar societies that lack mixed categories, such as Rwanda and Burundi, are the most likely to have genocide. The main preventive measure at this early stage is to develop universalistic institutions that transcend ethnic or racial divisions, that actively promote tolerance and understanding, and that promote classifications that transcend the divisions. The Catholic church could have played this role in Rwanda, had it not been driven by the same ethnic cleavages as Rwandan society. Promotion of a common language in countries like Tanzania has also promoted transcendent national identity. This search for common ground is vital to early prevention of genocide.

2. **SYMBOLIZATION**: We give names or other symbols to the classifications. We name people "Jews" or "Gypsies," or distinguish them by colors or dress, and apply the symbols to members of groups. Classification and symbolization are universally human and do not necessarily result in genocide unless they lead to the next stage—dehumanization. When combined with hatred, symbols may be forced upon unwilling members of pariah groups: the yellow star for Jews under Nazi rule, the blue scarf for people from the Eastern Zone in Khmer Rouge Cambodia. To combat symbolization, hate symbols can be legally forbidden (swastikas), as can hate speech. Group marking like gang clothing or tribal scarring can be outlawed, as well. The problem is that legal limitations will fail if unsupported by popular cultural enforcement. Though Hutu and Tutsi were forbidden words in Burundi until the 1980s, code words replaced them. If widely supported, however, denial of symbolization can be powerful, as it was

in Bulgaria, where the government refused to supply enough yellow badges, and at least eighty percent of Jews did not wear them, depriving the yellow star of its significance as a Nazi symbol for Jews.

3. **DEHUMANIZATION**: One group denies the humanity of the other group. Members of it are equated with animals, vermin, insects, or diseases. Dehumanization overcomes the normal human revulsion against murder. At this stage, hate propaganda in print and on hate radios is used to vilify the victim group. In combating this dehumanization, incitement to genocide should not be confused with protected speech. Genocidal societies lack constitutional protection for countervailing speech and should be treated differently than democracies. Local and international leaders should condemn the use of hate speech and make it culturally unacceptable. Leaders who incite genocide should be banned from international travel and have their foreign finances frozen. Hate radio stations should be shut down, and hate propaganda banned. Hate crimes and atrocities should be promptly punished.

4. **ORGANIZATION**: Genocide is always organized, usually by the state, often using militias to provide deniability of state responsibility (the Janjaweed in Darfur). Sometimes organization is informal (Hindu mobs led by local RSS militants) or decentralized (terrorist groups). Special army units or militias are often trained and armed. Plans are made for genocidal killings. To combat this stage, membership in these militias should be outlawed. Their leaders should be denied visas for foreign travel. The U.N. should impose arms embargoes on governments and citizens of countries involved in genocidal massacres, and create commissions to investigate violations, as was done in post-genocide Rwanda.

5. **POLARIZATION**: Extremists drive the groups apart. Hate groups broadcast polarizing propaganda. Laws may forbid intermarriage or social interaction. Extremist terrorism targets moderates, intimidating and silencing the center. Moderates from the perpetrators' own group are most able to stop genocide, and so are the first to be arrested and killed. Prevention may mean security protection for moderate leaders or assistance to human rights groups. Assets of extremists may be seized, and visas for international travel denied to them. Coup d'états by extremists should be opposed by international sanctions.

6. **PREPARATION**: Victims are identified and separated out because of their ethnic or religious identity. Death lists are drawn up. Members of victim groups are forced to wear identifying symbols. Their property is expropriated. They are often segregated into ghettoes, deported into concentration camps, or confined to a famine-struck region and starved. At this stage, a Genocide Emergency must be declared. If the political will of the great powers, regional alliances, or the U.N. Security Council can be mobilized, armed international intervention should be prepared, or heavy assistance provided to the victim group to prepare for its self-defense. Otherwise, at least humanitarian assistance should be organized by the U.N. and private relief groups for the inevitable tide of refugees to come.

7. **EXTERMINATION** begins and quickly becomes the mass killing legally called "genocide." It is "extermination" to the killers because they do not believe their victims to be fully human. When it is sponsored by the state, the armed forces often work with militias to do the killing. Sometimes the genocide results in revenge killings by groups against each other, creating the downward whirl-pool-like cycle of bilateral genocide (as in Burundi). At this stage, only rapid and overwhelming armed intervention can stop genocide. Real safe areas or refugee escape corridors should be established with heavily armed international protection. (An unsafe "safe" area is worse than none at all.) The U.N. Standing High Readiness Brigade, EU Rapid Response Force, or regional forces—should be authorized to act by the U.N. Security Council if the genocide is small. For larger interventions, a multilateral force authorized by the U.N. should intervene. If the U.N. is paralyzed, regional alliances must act. It is time to recognize that the international responsibility to protect transcends the narrow interests of individual nation states. If strong nations will not provide troops to intervene directly, they should provide the airlift, equipment, and financial means necessary for regional states to intervene.

8. **DENIAL** is the eighth stage that always follows a genocide. It is among the surest indicators of further genocidal massacres. The perpetrators of genocide dig up the mass graves, burn the bodies, try to cover up the evidence, and intimidate the witnesses. They deny that they committed any crimes, and often blame what happened on the victims. They block investigations of the crimes, and continue to govern until driven from power by force, when they flee into exile. There they remain with impunity, like Pol Pot or Idi Amin, unless they are captured and a

tribunal is established to try them. The response to denial is punishment by an international tribunal or national courts. There the evidence can be heard and the perpetrators punished. Tribunals like the Yugoslav or Rwanda Tribunals, or an international tribunal to try the Khmer Rouge in Cambodia, or an International Criminal Court, may not deter the worst genocidal killers. But with the political will to arrest and prosecute them, some may be brought to justice.

Prevent: Individual Activity
The 5 C's

Students: In the blank box below, write a word or a sentence that describes "you" in each of the five categories. *For ex. Color: "Light skin, female, 16." Culture: "I am Asian; I speak two languages; I love Wendy's cheeseburgers." Clout: "I have my own money from babysitting." Character: "I can sing; I want to be a psychiatrist; I hate gossip; I believe in marriage." Context: "I live in a two-story house in the city with my family."*

5 C's	Example	Describe "You"
Color	Characteristics you're born with and usually can't change such as: Skin Color, Physical Size, Gender, Age.	
Culture	Characteristics of the group you identify with such as: Food, Language, Race/Religion, Beliefs.	
Clout	The amount of power, status, and influence you have such as: Economic Status, Social Status, Power.	
Character	These characteristics represent your personality traits such as: Talents, Abilities, Skills, Goals.	
Context	This determines where, when, and whom you live with such as: Town, State, Generation, Family.	

Prevent: Group Activity—The 5 C's

Students: Now that you have your five categories filled out from the **Individual Activity**, compare your characteristics to another person's characteristics in your class. In the blank box below, list some shared characteristics between you both. *For ex., do you share the same skin color, same age, and same gender? Do you like the same foods, speak the same language? Does anyone else want the same future career as you? Does anyone else know how to sing, dance, and play a certain sport that you do? Do you and the other person have only one younger brother or a single mother or grandparents living with them?*

5 C's	Example	Student #1	Student #2
Color	Characteristics you're born with and usually can't change such as: Skin Color, Physical Size, Gender, Age.		
Culture	Characteristics of the group you identify with such as: Food, Language, Race/Religion, Beliefs.		
Clout	The amount of power, status, and influence you have such as: Economic Status, Social Status, Power.		
Character	These characteristics represent your personality traits such as: Talents, Abilities, Skills, Goals.		
Context	This determines where, when, and whom you live with such as: Town, State, Generation, Family.		

Group Activity Alternative: The Line Game

This can be used as a physical activity in conjunction with the above 5 C's or alone. The Line Game is a diversity exercise that requires everyone in the class to stand on one side of the room. The facilitator asks anyone in line to cross to the other side of the room if they share the following characteristics; for example: "Cross the room if you . . . "

1. are wearing shoes with laces;
2. are wearing anything black;
3. have a dog;
4. have a cat;
5. have one parent;
6. have siblings;
7. have broken a bone;
8. have lied to a friend;
9. laughed at someone;
10. felt laughed at yourself;
11. defended someone against gossip or lies;
12. wished someone had stood up for you.

For more examples see our Resources section or gather everyone's 5 C's cards and make a list of common characteristics your students share. For additional guidelines on how to facilitate this exercise check out our online Resources.

Combat: Group Activity
Threat Level Assessment

Low-Risk

The Haters' Club website or social networking profile shows up with a few mild insults posted about you. It doesn't show any photos of you or identifying information other than your student's name. What do you do?

_____

_____

_____

_____

_____

_____

_____

Guarded Risk

The Haters' Club website or social networking profile displays your name, your face, and is using information you posted about yourself online against you in every mean and nasty way possible. It is still up after twenty-four hours of reporting it and nothing has changed. More negative anonymous comments are added daily. What do you do?

_____

_____

_____

_____

_____

_____

_____

Elevated Risk

The Haters' Club website or social networking profile goes full-force with multiple people joining as a gang of bullies. The bullies use tactics like flaming, harassment, rumors, and ridicule. Their language is abusive, profane, or posts your personal info (email address, phone number) to encourage more abuse. What do you do?

_____

_____

_____

_____

_____

_____

_____

High-Risk

The bullies encourage others to post "hate speech" (any words targeting your race, gender, disability, or sexual orientation) or make statements to provoke others to stalk and harass the you; or—post threatening comments saying you will be hurt or killed. What do you do?

_____

_____

_____

_____

_____

_____

_____

five

Cell Phone Tactics: Sexting

Sexting:

To send a text message to someone containing sexual messages or sexually explicit photos.

In this tactic, the target bears the responsibility of sending a nude and/or explicitly sexualized photo of himself or herself by cell phone or digital camera to a romantic partner. When the relationship ends, the recipient of this photo may turn into the perpetrator deliberately by forwarding the photo electronically to other recipients or posting the photos publicly on the Internet. An innocent recipient may also become an unwitting perpetrator by forwarding the photo electronically to the authorities. In other cases, a third party can be the perpetrator. For example, someone finds or hijacks the cell phone containing the Sexting photo, then circulates it by cell phone or uploads it to a website, unbeknownst to either the sender or recipient of the photo.

Getting Started

Lesson Rundown   Students are introduced to the concept of Sexting in which an explicitly sexual photo of oneself is forwarded to friends or romantic partners. The photos can potentially be uploaded to a website to humiliate the target.

Objective   Students will be able to:

- understand what motivates someone to want to take a Sexting photo and the consequences of doing so;
- make deliberate choices to limit what types of photographs are allowed to be taken and uploaded by friends;
- practice "collaborative negotiation" between two people in a relationship;
- internalize the concept of facing the fear, finding allies, and re-assessing one's motivations in the aftermath of a Sexting incident.

Time Needed   The Understand, Combat, and Transform sections are structured to be conducted within a typical classroom requiring 30-40 minutes of lesson time. The Prevent sections may require 30-60 minutes as they go more in-depth and may prompt more conversation. Total estimated time for the Sexting Unit is 2-3 hours and will vary in an after-school or workshop environment.

Teacher Prep   Review any group or individual activities ahead of time for materials needed to maximize in-class time.

Equipment/
Supplies Needed   Computers with Internet access can be used for high-tech activities. Otherwise, paper and writing materials can be used for low-tech activities.

Vocab Words   Defined at the end of this section.

Handouts   *Group Activity: Collaborative Negotiation; Sample Memorandum of Understanding; Threat Level Assessments*

For The Educator

Tactic Overview

Our goal with this tactic is to provide teachers and students with a little more understanding about how and why teens engage in Sexting, as well as provide student discussion topics and activities to minimize personal injury. Sexting will be a sensitive topic among a co-ed classroom, and very likely students will not feel very comfortable volunteering if they have ever known someone who has engaged in it (although privately they may come to you afterward). This lesson will help both boys and girls understand the devastating effects of submitting private photos to a "trusted" friend or romantic partner and how it can always be used against them. In this chapter, you will be able to teach them how to protect themselves against Sexting by being proactive about how they use their cell phones.

Sexting: Who's Doing It?: First, let's start with what everyone already knows. Tween/teen cell phone use has risen exponentially in recent years, and texting has become the primary way teens communicate. With the latest technology, photos and texts created through a smartphone are a click away from being immediately posted online to various outlets like Twitter, Facebook, and My Yahoo accounts, as well as to online photo galleries like Picasa, Flickr and Pinterest.

When we first started writing this book, we had no idea how dramatic the rise in teen cell phone use would be in just a few short years. A 2009 Pew Internet & American Life Project report, *Teens and Mobile Phones,* found that 75% of twelve-to seventeen-year-olds own cell phones, up from 45% in 2004; and the primary way teens communicate today is through cell phone texting.[84]

As far as how *prevalent* Sexting is, national estimates have varied considerably. In a nationally representative 2009 survey of twelve-to seventeen-year-olds conducted on landlines and cell phones, the Pew Research Center's Internet & American Life Project found that only:

- 4% of cell-owning teens ages 12-17 say they have sent sexually suggestive nude or nearly nude photos of themselves to someone else via text messaging; and
- 15% of cell-owning teens ages 12-17 say they have received sexually suggestive nude or nearly nude photos of someone they know via text messaging on their cell phone.[85]

In 2011, the authors of a national survey of 1,560 US 10-to-17-year-olds published in the medical journal *Pediatrics* say that only about 1% of kids admitted they had created sexually explicit images and 7.1% said they had received nude or nearly nude images of others.[86] These all seem like low numbers, yet a 2011 MTV-AP Digital Abuse Study reveals a dramatic increase in Sexting with one-third of teens (ages 14-24) admitting to have sent or received "Sext" messages on their phones or online. Further, 71 percent of the teens polled describe Sexting as a serious problem.[87]

Whether the students polled in the MTV-AP Digital Abuse Study were being more forthright with their answers than the kids polled in the other studies, we'll never know. The real issue is what do we do with the students who engage in and have been caught Sexting? First, let's get to the heart of what motivates teens to share explicit photos.

Fun? Or Social Pressure?

From the 2009 MTV-AP Digital Abuse Study, 31% of the teens surveyed reported that they have shared Sexts as "a joke."[88] But when you combine girls, social pressure, cell phones, and the law, there's nothing funny about Sexting. The National Campaign to Prevent Teen and Unplanned Pregnancy and a CosmoGirl.com survey revealed 51% of teen girls said pressure from a guy was a reason girls send sexy messages or photos, while only 18% of teen boys cited pressure from female counterparts as a reason.[89] The survey further revealed that 52% of teen girls did so as a "sexy present" for their boyfriend.[90]

Why It Happens

It comes down to the age-old negotiation between boys and girls—giving up something means getting something. Focus group findings from the Teens and Mobile Use study show that Sexting within a relationship occurs most often in one of three scenarios:

- between two romantic partners;
- between two romantic partners where the image then becomes shared outside the relationship;
- between people who are not yet in a relationship, but where often one person hopes to be.

The study goes on to illustrate that: "Teens explained how sexually suggestive images have become a form of relationship currency. These images are shared as a part of or instead of sexual activity, or as a way of starting or maintaining a relationship with a significant other. They are also passed along to friends for their entertainment value, as a joke, for revenge or for fun."[91]

Cyberbullying Sexting Vs. Experimental Sexting

There is a big difference between a consensual pact between two people and what happens when trickery, revenge, and blackmail are used in the malicious dissemination of photos. This is what Nancy Willard, MS, JD, Director of the Center for Safe and Responsible Internet Use, differentiates as "Cyberbullying Sexting." Her paper, *Sexting & Youth: Achieving a Rational Response*, aptly describes what happens when the wrong people with the wrong intentions get a hold of this very precious photographic "currency." Her paper describes at least four basic variations of this tactic:

- *Trickery:* The perpetrator creates an Imposter Profile of a "hot boy or girl" with the purpose of getting the target to willingly forward a Sext: sort of a digital variation of "I'll show you mine if you show me yours."

- *Blackmail:* The perpetrator either inadvertently finds an image on the target's cell phone and takes it without permission or uses a previously sent image that was sent within the duration of the relationship to get the target to do something in order to avoid dissemination of the image.

- *Photoshopping:* The perpetrator doesn't even need a real "body shot" of the target, just a "head shot" in which the two photographs are digitally spliced. The perpetrator now may disseminate the image in a variety of malicious ways and, until it is too late, the target is none the wiser.

- *Revenge Porn:* This term Willard, borrowed from Urban Dictionary defines it as: "Homemade porn uploaded by ex-girlfriend or (usually) ex-boyfriend after a particularly vicious breakup as a means of humiliating the ex or just for own amusement."[92]

Different Consequences For Boys And Girls

The assumption with Sexting is that girls who disseminate sexual photos bear the fallout far worse than boys, but each gender bears a heavy burden. For girls, the emotional impact of being humiliated by a circulating image, not just once, but over and over, due to the viral nature of the Internet, can be devastating, particularly when it mutates offline into social ridicule, sexual harassment, and public shaming. This is known as **"slut-shaming"** and is a powerful social tactic to impugn a girl's character in order to demean her. For boys, the risk they take in exchanging Sexting photos has criminal consequences. "They are the ones who will be arrested, prosecuted, and required to register as a sex offender," says Willard. "One day, 'boys will be boys'—the next, they are registered sexual offenders and their life is destroyed.[93]

Scenario
Aaliyah's Story

Print the below story and hand out to the students. For more interactivity, assign someone to read it to the entire class.

For Everyone's Eyes Only

When Aaliyah started getting the attention of Lavon, her older brother's best friend, she was thirteen and he was seventeen. Lavon texted her at least twenty times that week and she loved the attention, even when he teased her by texting: "Ur 2 young." Aaliyah wanted to prove that she wasn't and tried to act older when she was around him. Several weeks later, Lavon asked Aaliyah to send him a special photo, for his eyes only. She couldn't explain why, but it bothered Aaliyah that he asked. Her own brother constantly looked at nasty stuff on the Internet when their parents weren't around, and she didn't like it. One of her friends, Ashlee, had an older boyfriend, and as a pact Ashlee and her boyfriend had been sharing naked photos of themselves . . . a secret little thrill to keep the relationship strong. There were too many girls out there who'd be just as willing to "steal her boyfriend," Ashlee warned, so sending these pics were her "insurance."

When Aaliyah snapped the photos of herself, she felt really guilty and could barely look at them. She debated a long time before sending them to Lavon, but the final push came when Ashlee IM'd her that there was a rumor going on that Lavon might be interested in someone else. Click. Send. "These r ONLY 4 u. Dont show these 2 any1," she texted Lavon. "PLEASE."

Two days later, Ashlee told Aaliyah there was a website all the boys were looking at with Aaliyah's name and the caption, "She may be H-O-T, but she's still a H-O." Aaliyah felt immediately sick to her stomach. She couldn't believe it. When she got online and clicked on the link, she went completely cold. Scrolling down the photos, she began to cry. She couldn't tell her mom or the principal—nobody could know! She felt humiliated, especially after all those horrible things they were saying about her in the comments section. All she could hope for is that they wouldn't spread around to the entire school, but of course that didn't happen. The next day, in between classes, people in the hallways threw pencils at her. Two girls called her a "slut" to her face. Aaliyah immediately accused Lavon of betraying her, but he acted as though he'd done nothing wrong. Within another day, her mother got a concerned call from a teacher at school, who'd been notified of the site with Aaliyah's photos. When the police had been notified, Lavon was immediately arrested and an investigation had begun. Then the local newspapers picked up the story. The police were trying to determine whether Lavon had set up the website himself or, when he mass-forwarded the photos to his friends, if someone else had done it. Not only was Aaliyah completely devastated by what had happened to her, but now she was in legal trouble for sending the photo of herself through her cell phone. She was suspended from school—but that wasn't the worst of it. Now her story had made the local news and everyone was talking about it!

Step I: Understand

Objective   Students will be able to:
- identify all the negative consequences that go with participating in this tactic, including criminal penalties;
- understand why girls are motivated to send photos of themselves and what motivates boys to ask;
- understand how "disengaged onlookers" contribute to the bullying aspect of this tactic.

Time Needed   55 minutes.

Teacher Prep   Copy handouts of the Scenario for the class or display through a wall projector and have students vocalize the roles of the characters.

Equipment/ Supplies Needed   Copier. Computers with Internet access (high-tech) or paper and pencils (low-tech).

Vocab Words   Defined at the end of this section.

Overview

Start with the Topic for Discussion to get students warmed up. Gradually move on to show them the various roles people play in this particular tactic.

Establish Group Guidelines   See the guidelines in **Appendix C** in order to get the most out of your group discussions in class.

Topic for Discussion   Young people know that sending sexually explicit content through digital media inevitably has negative consequences, but they do it anyway. Ask your students if they've ever heard of the term, "**slut-shaming**." In an informal poll, ask students to list all the potential negative consequences of Sexting for girls. Now list them for the boys. Are these consequences equal?

Define Tactic   Determine the maturity of your class before introducing this chapter, and define what Sexting is to your students, perhaps after using the informal survey in **Appendix A**. Many of them will most likely have already heard of this term, but surprisingly some students will have not.

For The Student: A   Online conflict isn't always clear-cut. Once you've gotten through
Broader Perspective   the Topic For Discussion, go over the roles of each participant in the scenario with your class. We've provided multiple perspectives to help students gain insight.

From The Bully's Perspective: Lavon claimed he wasn't the one who set up the website that featured Aaliyah's explicit photos, but several things are clear. He was the recipient of these texted photos, and rather than delete them to protect Aaliyah, he treated them as trophies or status symbols to be shared among his friends. In doing so, he was charged with what law enforcement deems "producing, directing, or promoting a photograph featuring the sexual conduct of a child."[94] He was served with an extra count of possession of child pornography. Completely unaware that Aaliyah was also breaking the law by sending these photos of herself, Lavon unwittingly engaged in digital child pornography trafficking by merely forwarding the photos via cell phone to his friends.

From The Target's Perspective: Girls need to be even more aware of the consequences to Sexting; ignorance will only set them up for disaster later. "Teens tend to not think twice about texting a sexually graphic photo to their boyfriend or girlfriend," says cyber crime expert Jayne A. Hitchcock. "They don't realize that the person they send it to is probably going to forward it, and it *will* end up online. These teens are not stupid. They're smart kids—but they're naive and very trusting. They trust their boyfriend or girlfriend to keep the photo to themselves and, of course, that's not going to happen."[95]

Aaliyah's home life could be described as "at-risk" and she sometimes turned to chat rooms for attention. She didn't understand that her real value came from her thoughts, her actions, and her character, not her body. Once she clicked SEND those photos became like a virus, spreading everywhere through cell phones, blogs, and websites. To this day, the police and families of the boys were able to delete most of the photos, but Aaliyah had good cause to fear that not all of them were scrubbed and that they'd someday come back again to haunt her online.

From The Follower's Perspective: Aaliyah's friend Ashlee didn't consider herself an accomplice to the bully. However, her naive advice in convincing Aaliyah to send Lavon that photo as "insurance" made her into an unwitting follower, something every girl's best friend ought to be aware of when it comes to this tactic. Likewise, the "friend" of Lavon's who'd set up the website anonymously is another example of a follower. While this friend was having fun humiliating Aaliyah, he was also contributing to Lavon's eventual arrest.

From The Supporters' Perspective: Of all the students at Lavon and Aaliyah's school who viewed this anonymous website, some followers took an active role in the cyberbullying just by simply commenting on the photos. Others, who viewed the website but didn't comment, still supported the bully by being **disengaged onlookers**. Their position was "It's not my business" and they didn't take a stand. Disengaged onlookers always reserve the right not to do anything, but we use **"The Golden Rule"** whenever faced with this question, "If you were about to be humiliated not just in your school and community but *nationally*—would you want someone to go out of their way to help you?"

Group Activity	*High-tech:* Allow small groups to gather around a computer or computers with wireless Internet and access www.thatsnotcool.com. Click on Videos and "Two Sided Stories" and have them watch "Pressure Pic Problem." Ask the boys to watch the video on the left hand side of the screen and girls to watch the video on the right hand of the screen. Have them answer the built-in quiz for each video, and then scroll down to the comment section to see what other kids have said. Note: some of the language in these videos is more for a high school audience.

Low-tech: If you don't have access to a computer, then go to the site beforehand, www.thatsnotcool.com and click on the tab "Talk It Out." Click on "Pic Pressure" topic icon on the left then print out **screenshots** of some of the advice real teens have given. Note: though this site is designed for teens, the comment section offers very real (re: not always filtered) advice from teens to teens about Sexting. Ask your small groups to analyze the teen advice and discuss whether it is valuable or not.

Virginia high school senior Mayron G. says a nude photo that she heard a girl sent her boyfriend showed up on her phone last year. "The whole class was sharing it by the end of the day. The guys said, 'She's so hot.' The girls were more like, 'I feel sorry for the girl,' or they just lost all respect for her."[96]

Teacher Takeaway Tip

Depending on the age and maturity of your students, you may, at your discretion, let them know that using drugs or alcohol and taking cell phone photos are a bad combination, according to several students who'd revealed to us that's how it happened to them. Because of the lowered inhibition, many teens who "didn't remember" posing a certain way find themselves a target when a friend or enemy posts the photos online. In this hyper-digital age, especially with facial recognition software sure to be available in a matter of years, be wary of the camera at all times under the influence.

VOCAB WORDS

Disengaged Onlookers: Those who watch what happens but do not take a stand.

Slut-Shaming: Calling a girl or woman a "slut" or a "whore" or impugning her character in sexual terms in order to embarrass, humiliate, intimidate, degrade, or shame her for actions or behaviors.

The Golden Rule: Behave toward others as you would like to have them behave toward you.

Step II: Prevent

Objective	Students will be able to:

Students will be able to:

- analyze the emotional factors that lead to Sexting;
- understand male and female motivations for taking and sending Sexting photos;
- work on "collaborative negotiation" to give both parties what they want without involving Sexting;
- protect both parties with behavioral and technological strategies to prevent being the target of Sexting.

Time Needed   30-60 minutes.

Teacher Prep   Go over conflict resolution concepts with the class. Distribute handouts.

Equipment/ Supplies Needed   A computer lab and printer would be beneficial for this section, but the individual and group activity can both be done in low-tech classrooms.

Vocab Words   Defined at the end of this section.

For The Parents: Cell Phone Monitoring Software

According to a Nielsen Mobile Kids Insights study in 2009, "more than half of parents do not apply any parental controls offered by service providers to their children's cell phone usage— although the use of these paid-for controls is increasing."[97] There is still controversy over whether parents should "stealth monitor" a teenager's cell phone, because doing so erodes the teenager's trust, but experts agree that in extreme cases the invasion of privacy outweighs the child's rights when his or her health and safety are at risk. Regardless, parents need to put the same guidelines around a teenager's cell phone use exactly the way they do around a home computer and be aware of what kind of communication is transpiring on the teenager's cell phone.

We're choosing to include cell phone access advice here so parents know what all of their options are. For a monthly fee of roughly ten dollars, parents can load monitoring software such as My Mobile Watchdog (www.mymobilewatchdog.com) and Mobile Spy (www.mobile-spy.com) into the teen's cell phone, and then create a list of contacts who are authorized to access the cell phone. All activity on the teen's cell phone then goes to an online file, which the parent can access, showing all text messages and shared photos. If any unauthorized caller contacts the teen's cell phone, the parent will receive a real-time text message alert. This includes if the teen has removed the software from his or her cell phone. See our online Resources for more cell phone monitoring recommendations.

For The Educator: Conflict Resolution Concepts

Now that the students have identified the roles of bullies, targets, and bystanders, it is time to **"post-play"** the opening scenario to get your students to understand how to problem solve when two people have strong but differing needs. In this tactic, we will focus on **Collaborative Negotiation**, particularly between two people in a relationship where "Sexting" is a possibility.

Let's focus again on the main players in the above scenario. Lavon had underlying needs for wanting Aaliyah's nude photos, just as she had underlying needs to send them to him. In the previous activities and discussions, it should be clear that his needs and hers were vastly in conflict. "Negotiation works best when the disputants view themselves as partners trying to solve a problem, not as individuals on opposing sides," say authors Girard and Koch of *Conflict Negotiation in the Schools*.[98] Bodine, Crawford, and Schrumpf, the authors of *Creating The Peaceable School* (qtd in *Conflict Resolution in the Schools*) contend that to negotiate collaboratively, each person "is an empathic listener, suspends judgment, is respectful, and has a cooperative spirit."[99]

The following is *Creating The Peaceable School's* model of Collaborative Negotiation. Picture Lavon and Aaliyah as the participants following these six steps:

1. **Agree to negotiate**: The two participants must be willing to hear each other's point of view and work toward a solution that is fair and satisfying to both.

2. **Gather points of view**: Each participant must identify with one another's underlying needs and interests and practice active listening to "put himself or herself in the other person's shoes."

3. **Find common interests**: Each participant must find common ground. At the very least, each participant has a shared need to avoid the consequences if they fail to reach resolution.

4. **Create win-win options**: Think of all possible solutions for both participants to have mutual gain. Work on generating lots of possibilities; don't criticize any yet.

5. **Evaluate options**: Look at the best of the brainstormed possibilities based on what's most fair to both participants.

6. **Formalizing the agreement**: Each side then tells the other what he or she is willing to do. This could also be a jointly-written **memorandum of understanding**.[100]

Individual Activity   *High-tech:* Go To MTV's "A Thin Line" (www.athinline.org) website and click on the Sexting tab. Allow the students to read real questions from other students across the country facing Sexting pressures in the Archives. Ask students to write "big brother" or "big sister" advice to the younger students in school about the following question in a notebook or on 3 x 5 index cards.

My boyfriend took nude photos of me, and now that we have broken up he refuses to delete them. What can I do?[101]

Low-tech: Have students write "big brother" or "big sister" advice to the younger students in school about the same question above in a notebook or on 3 x 5 index cards.

Self-Defense   On the board, write down two columns: **Behavior** and **Tech Defense**. Ask your class to volunteer their own suggestions to prevent being the target of Sexting and follow up by presenting the strategies below.

Behavior

There is no guaranteed way to protect one's image online once it has been uploaded. The poster can remove it, but someone else might have already downloaded it prior to its removal. And once that happens, the image can be manipulated, posted repeatedly to websites, cell phones, and other devices, and may never be completely scrubbed from cyberspace.

Here are some behavioral suggestions for students to protect themselves from becoming a target of this Sexting tactic.

- **Assess Underlying Motivation**: Examine your motivations behind wanting to send nude or semi-nude photos of yourself or what's really at stake when you ask someone else to. Try to analyze your own reasons and impulses for wanting to do this. Is this your idea or is someone pressuring you? Are you sending it as a joke? To gain someone's attention? To hurt someone? And do you know for sure where it will end up, or do you just have someone's "promise" it won't be shared? Before you are ever tempted to try it, list the pros and cons of doing it vs. not doing it.

- **Don't Drink/Drug 'N Sext**: For the older students in your classroom, this is advice right from our own teens. Never engage in drinking or other drugs in combination with digital self-expression. Our research revealed that kids who admitted doing this were in no state to understand that photos of them had been taken or posted online.

- **Pays to Be Paranoid**: All of your social networking photos should pass the "Would I Be Embarrassed If This Photo Got Out?" test. Never take or send out photos of yourself or allow others to take photos that are embarrassing, inappropriate, or overly sexualized. Always remember that one photo in the wrong hands can change the content of the photo's meaning instantly.

- **Let Your Friends Be The Judge**: After this chapter, you should get together with a small group of your closest friends and play a game. Allow them to look at every photo you've saved on your phone. Like a group of judges on American Idol, they get to tell you whether the photos pass the "Pays To Be Paranoid" test . . . or not. If there are any photos on your phone you wouldn't feel comfortable showing even your closest friends, that is your strongest clue to delete them . . . now!

- **Friend Pact**: Have all your friends make a "**friend pact**" that no one will ever upload another's photo without permission. They should *always* ask you before uploading any photos of you and they should *never* post any photos of you that are negative or compromising. Be vigilant about watching out for each other's photos on the 'Net.

- **Parent Pact**: Show your parents they can trust you by making a cell phone pact with them. Though you may not like this suggestion, if you want to have the privilege of owning a cell phone, you ought to be able to show the responsibility that goes with it. Many parents have the power and control to oversee what you are texting and who you are calling anyway—especially if they are paying the cell phone bills. So prove to your parents that if they "check" the photos on your cell phone at any given time—they won't have anything to worry about. You also have a built-in excuse to anyone who asks you to send a Sext by saying, "I can't. My parents look at what's on my phone."

Tech Defense

In a computer lab these exercises can be easily done in a class period, depending on the amount of time everyone has. This is an excellent exercise to help students get familiar with how technology can aid them before they ever experience cyberbullying.

- **Monitor All Your Photos Online**: Create a **Google Alert** with your real name and any nicknames you're known by.[102] A Google Alert scours the web for any information with the keywords you plug in and delivers the content back to the student via email. Consider adding additional words like SEX, NUDE, HOT, NAKED, PIX, etc. in combination with your name to strengthen this search. If someone has posted your image with your name attached, an email will come to your inbox and you will be the first to know.

- **Profile Image Management**: Be mindful of not only in the type of photos you upload yourself, but especially what your friends and boyfriend/girlfriends (who can always turn out to be potential enemies) upload of you. Even with social profiles set to private, photos can be "**tagged**" and posted publicly somewhere else.

- **TigerText**: Be aware that this app for iPhones allows sent text messages to be deleted on demand or to vanish after a specific time period. These messages cannot be saved, copied or forwarded by recipients. On the one hand, this app can protect you from having evidence of a stupid mistake land in the wrong hands. On the other hand, this app can be used for malicious cyberbullying purposes—and evidence cannot be preserved.[103]

Group Activity   Break students into two groups, one representing Aaliyah and one representing Lavon. Ask the groups to look at each of the six steps of Collaborative Negotiation in the handout at the end of this chapter and write a list of practical suggestions and advice as it relates to Aaliyah and Lavon. If the collaborative negotiation is successful, consider drawing up a Memorandum of Understanding for your whole class (see handout at the end of this chapter). If it is unsuccessful, stop and ask the students to discuss where the breakdown of negotiation occurred in the six steps.

For The Educator

We've provided possible answers to go with this activity so that you know what to look for.

Agree to negotiate: Each group can assume both Aaliyah and Lavon are willing to negotiate and talk to one another.

Gather points of view: What do they both want/really need that has nothing to do with sex or a photo?

[Possible answers: respect, commitment, attraction, love, status, etc.]

Find common interests: What are other common interests of boys and girls in a relationship apart from sex?

[Possible answers: family, culture, hobbies, friendship, music, TV shows, movies, etc.]

Create win-win options: List possible solutions for Aaliyah and Lavon to both get what they want without Sexting. List at least three possible solutions each.

[Possible answers: agree to be exclusive, agree to be physical up to a point, agree not to send regular photos of themselves to any other boy/girl, etc.]

Evaluate options: Now look at that list above. Which possible solutions are the most fair to both Aaliyah and Lavon?

[Have students in each group pick the best two.]

Formalize the agreement: If each group was able to come up with enough solutions to sign the Memorandum of Understanding at the end of this chapter, then appoint someone in each group to fill in the blanks and sign it. If the exercise was unsuccessful, ask the groups to analyze why.

VOCAB WORDS

Collaborative Negotiation: In collaborative negotiation, the approach is to treat the relationship as just as important as the agreement.

Friend Pact: A formal agreement made and signed by two or more friends.

Google Alert: A content-monitoring service, offered by the search engine company Google, that automatically notifies users when new content from news, web, blogs, video, and/or discussion groups matches a set of search terms selected by the user.

Memorandum of Understanding: A legal document outlining the terms and details of an agreement between parties.

Post-Play: In "role-playing" this means analyzing what happened in the game (or scenario) after it has happened to know what to do in the event of a similar situation next time.

Tagged: In computer terminology, a tag is a term assigned to a piece of information such as a digital image. In this case, a person's real name is "tagged" or captioned under a digital image.

Step III: Combat

Objective   Students will be able to:

- identify low- to high-risk online situations;
- assess possible solutions to remedy conflict without resorting to revenge;
- practice making thoughtful, deliberate choices on how to react to the threat.

Time Needed   30 minutes.

Teacher Prep   Read any section ahead of class time labeled "For the Educator." Make a copy each of the Threat Level Assessments to hand out to four small groups.

Equipment/   Copier for handouts and paper and pencils for students.
Supplies Needed

Vocab Words   Defined at the end of this section.

In the following section we use our own version of the US Department of Defense's concept of "Threat Levels" when providing students action steps to take.

Note: the advice in this section does not purport to be legal advice. We have consulted with cyberbullying and Sexting experts to help parents and students know what to do in a Sexting situation.

Immediate Steps To Take

Many parents, educators, and school administrators only become aware of Sexting incidents when an explicit photo has already been circulated. Of all the tactics in this workbook, we urge school districts to be preemptive about implementing a cyberbullying policy specifically around Sexting. Coordinating with the local state's attorneys and law enforcement on its guidelines and parameters prior to any incidents is paramount, as any improper handling of Sexting "evidence" could land the recipient in severe legal trouble.[104]

If your teen has sent a Sext

"The worst thing parents can do is freak out," says noted cyber crime expert and Sexting author, Jayne A. Hitchcock. "The teen is already upset enough and needs to know she can go to her parent(s) for help if something like this happens. Parents should let their teen talk, show them where the photos ended up, whether it's on an online social networking site, message board, blog, or someone's website. Let the teen know that yes, what she did was wrong, but both the parent and teen need to work together to resolve the situation and make sure it never happens again."[105]

Depending on how explicit the photo is (showing any nudity) and if the teen is under eighteen, the moment one discovers a Sexting image, one must take great care because the teen can be charged with possession of child pornography—even if it is a self-portrait. Although parents may feel pressure not to report a Sexting incident, most experts agree doing nothing and "hoping it will die down" will only increase the chances of the photo going viral and increase the legal liability of everyone who knew about its existence. Because of the sexual content, it is very likely to get shared. MTV's digital dating abuse campaign, "A Thin Line" has found more than 50% of those who shared a Sext shared it with multiple people.[106]

However, legal experts recommend parents weigh the potential outcomes of going directly to the police based on the severity of the photos, the ages of the target/perpetrators/distributors, and whether the target is getting harassed because of it, among other factors. Because the legal issues of Sexting differ completely from state to state, parents have a legitimate concern about reporting Sexting photos to the authorities when the lawmakers of one state consider the act a "youthful mistake" and others consider it "a criminal act of child pornography." Some states are attempting to reconfigure state child-pornography law so that minors don't get charged with a felony and are forced to register as sex offenders as long as the incident was done voluntarily and without coercion.[107] In factoring your decision on what to do, be sure to know your state laws.

In some cases, law enforcement *must get involved*. For example, when Sexting is used to extort or pressure someone into doing something he or she wouldn't otherwise do or when the Sext has been forwarded to multiple people and there is no way to contain the situation or when an adult encourages a minor to send sexually explicit photos—these are all situations when the police will be involved regardless.[108] Your cooperation early on may be the only thing that lessens your legal trouble.

If your teen has received a Sext

Let's look at a classic scenario where an unwitting recipient opens his phone and discovers a Sext. Say a football player receives a private Sexting photo from his under-aged girlfriend meant only for him. In this scenario, the two break up and the football player decides, out of anger, to send the girl's nude image to every player on his football team. The innocent teammate, who now happens to open his phone and see this Sexting image, instantly has several choices: keep it and show it to others (including authorities) or delete it. What's the most prudent course of action?

While law enforcement generally contends that all evidence should always be reported, the innocent recipient of a Sexting photo faces a troubling Catch-22 predicament. Sexting experts believe that an innocent possessor of the image hasn't done anything illegal by merely *receiving* a Sext. It's what he chooses to do next that can minimize or maximize his legal exposure. If the possessor chooses to send or forward the Sexting image to a trusted adult thinking he's "doing the right thing," believe it or not, even with the best intentions, he now can be charged with distribution of child pornography. This is wholly unfair to the innocent possessor, particularly when state attorneys and law officials haven't proven across the board yet that they will always act sensibly and rationally in the face of discovering a Sext. Legislation around criminal behavior using technology against a person or targeted group is in varying stages in each state and not yet consistent at the federal level. Too often, overreaction replaces common sense when it comes to dealing with the "punishment" over these photos. Justin W. Patchin, PhD, Co-Director, Cyberbullying Research Center and Associate Professor of Criminal Justice at the University of Wisconsin-Eau Claire recommends: "My advice to teens who receive a nude or semi-nude image of a classmate is simple: immediately delete it. Don't tell anyone about it. If there is an investigation and someone asks if you received the image, you should tell them yes, but that you immediately deleted it."[109]

Illinois attorney Joshua Herman, who has published analysis and guidance regarding various Sexting issues, also suggests that the innocent possessor immediately delete the Sexting image. Doing so, says Herman, supports the defense in a child pornography case that the possessor is innocent. Time is of the essence, however. Herman points out that if the recipient carries the Sexting image around on his phone for two months and only deletes it when he learns that everyone else is getting busted, his legal position is vastly weakened. The innocent possessor is in the best position when he immediately deletes the image; but—departing from Patchin's advice, Herman says do report the situation to a parent or school official after the image is deleted so that the situation will resolve in the best manner possible.[110]

School officials, however, don't usually have a choice when discovering Sexting photos. Any school staff who discovers the photos may be required under certain state laws to report the photos to authorities the moment they are presented with the image—at the risk of keeping his or her job.[111] Furthermore, it is imperative for school staff and officials to be excruciatingly careful when discovering a Sexting image to not copy and save, forward, or store on anyone else's computer or phone at the risk of implicating themselves—as they do not have the same exemptions as law enforcement when it comes to collecting "evidence."[112]

Fill out Scene Survey

If you determine that you need to go to the police, take a **Scene Survey (Appendix B)** to gather as many facts and dates on paper as possible. Note: creating a Scene Survey for Sexting has different parameters than other chapters in this workbook due to the legal exposure one has in generating, transmitting, or possessing nude photos of minors. Again, school staff and officials *do not* have the same legal exemption in gathering and possessing Sexting photos as law enforcement. Therefore, do not try to copy and save or transmit any evidence of photos until the police have been consulted. Any attempts to "preserve evidence" or present the photos to the school authorities may in itself trigger criminal consequences.[113]

In the following Threat Level Assessment scenarios, parents would be wise to consult an attorney (and schools should be consulting their school attorney) on all situations above the hypothetical Low-Risk level.

Threat Level Assessment

In this section, the group activity comes before the lesson. This allows students to "pre-play" how they might react to each escalating situation. *Educators will need to make copies of the four Threat Level Assessments at the end of this chapter before the group activity can begin.*

Group Activity   Split the class into four small groups and ask them to retreat to each corner of the room. Assign each group a hypothetical situation ranging from Low-Risk to High-Risk (handouts found at the end of this chapter). Appoint a group leader to read the Threat Level Assessment on each handout to the group, and give each group a chance to write down their solutions to each hypothetical situation. After each group is done, ask the group leader (starting with Low Risk) to read the group's suggestions out loud to the class. Educators can provide the correct answer from the "What To Do" guide below for each Threat Level.

1. **Low-Risk**: You're over the age of eighteen and take a sexy (but not nude) photo of yourself, and then send it to your boyfriend, who is also eighteen or older. He does the same. The photos have not been seen or distributed to anyone else yet, but you have reasons to think they might soon.

    Frequency: This happens once.

    What To Do: This is a case where Sexting is consensual and not considered **"Cyberbullying Sexting."** With no nudity and of legal age, the target has not crossed any lines. However, that's not to say that unwanted distribution of this photo could occur with embarrassing consequences and other legal consequences if the relationship ends. While you are still on good terms with the significant other, say that you made a mistake and you want that the photo deleted immediately from all of the recipient's digital electronics (i.e. cell phone, computer, etc.). Make it very clear in writing that you do not give anyone permission to distribute that photo should it crop up on the Internet, and if it does that you will hold the recipient responsible.

2. **Guarded Risk**: You are under the age of eighteen and send a semi-nude photo (face showing) to someone also under eighteen. The image is only a day old but

has been sent around to two or three friends. So far, no evidence of the photos has been found online. However, someone's mom has found it and now has contacted your parents.

Frequency: The photos are now on multiple cell phones, but not yet on a website.

What To Do: Both the target and her family need to be very careful at this point because any electronic generation and transmission of nudity under the age of eighteen is considered criminal action. Depending on how long the recipients have possessed the image, if all parents and targets agree it might be best to delete the image to avoid having to go to the police. Herman states, "Finding and deleting an unsolicited Sext message an hour after its receipt better demonstrates involuntary possession than does carrying a Sext message on the phone for two months or more."[114]

But if there is even suspicion that one copy of that photo is still being electronically disseminated, the situation is now no longer containable on your own. Alert school administrators, then local law enforcement officers, who will carefully consider the target's alleged misconduct along with the perpetrator's and participating parties' alleged misconduct. As embarrassing as it may be, you will need to be proactive and closely monitor the situation, as it could get worse. If copies of the photos are found on anyone's phone or computer, that person could be arrested. Note: Any adult (parent or school official) who discovers the photo *should not* electronically forward the sexually explicit image (even as proof!) unless directed by law enforcement, or else face the unintended consequences of distributing child pornography himself or herself.[115] Parents and schools should, at this point, be consulting an attorney for legal guidance.

3. **Elevated Risk**: You are under the age of eighteen and have taken semi-nude photos of yourself (face showing) and sent it by cell phone to someone over eighteen, who has uploaded it to a social networking site or a website.

Frequency: The website has not yet been taken down. Negative or cruel comments are increasing, adding to the cyberbullying.

What To Do: Immediately contact the **Webmaster** to remove the image. Given the fact that the recipient is an adult, this is a clear-cut criminal offense. At this point, follow all the advice in Guarded Risk and contact local law enforcement officers so they can work with the target to get the image removed more quickly. If copies of the photos are found on anyone's phone or computer, that person could also be charged with child pornography. Do not electronically forward the sexually explicit image yourself. Follow advice directed by law enforcement. Do not try to hide evidence, but instead, be as cooperative as you can with the authorities in order to resolve the situation with the least amount of harm. Parents and schools should, at this point, be consulting an attorney for legal guidance.

4. **High-Risk**: You are under the age of eighteen and have taken explicit nude photos of yourself (some with face visible) with your cell phone but haven't sent them to anyone. Someone you don't know has retrieved them from your cell phone and has circulated them to multiple recipients. A public website/profile/blog is now featuring the photos online.

Frequency: The site has gone viral and harassment is happening offline because of it.

What To Do: There is no question that this situation is already out of the target's control, so immediately contact your local law enforcement officers who have been trained to carefully consider all angles of the alleged misconduct. They will consider a multitude of factors to get to the bottom of it, including determining who the **perpetrator** is and if the target is facing harassment because of her inappropriate behavior.[116] Save all evidence, including any interaction with the law and school. Do not show anyone or electronically forward the sexually explicit image. Follow advice directed by law enforcement and work with them to put a message out to the perpetrators, their parents, and all bystanders that if they participate in downloading or viewing these photos they may also be arrested, and perhaps even be registered as "sex offenders." Parents and schools should, at this point, be consulting an attorney for legal guidance.

Topic For Discussion   Now that everyone has had a chance to see how complicated a Sexting incident is, ask your students what they would do if they received a nude or semi-nude photo of an under-age teen on their phone or through email. What should they not do?

VOCAB WORDS

Cyberbullying Sexting: The taking of explicit sexual photos by a person under age eighteen in which the transmission and dissemination of the photos is not consensual, but instead done out of spite or revenge.

Perpetration: To do or perform something evil, criminal, or offensive.

Webmaster: An employee of the organization who is hosting the website you need to contact.

Step IV: Transform

Objective   Students will be able to:

- empathize with those who have made the mistake of Sexting;
- work on getting one's self-esteem back after becoming a target of Sexting;
- practice making thoughtful, deliberate choices on how to react after a Sexting incident;
- "pre-play" how they would deal with being asked for a Sexting photo in the future.

Time Needed   30 minutes.

Teacher Prep   Read any passage ahead of class time labeled "For the Educator."

Equipment/ Supplies Needed   Paper and pencils for students to take notes during Topic for Discussion.

Teacher Tip   This section is best absorbed if read first by the educator and used as a basis for a Topic For Discussion at the end. Though boys can be targets of this tactic, the majority of Sexting targets are girls. This section focuses on how they might transform the shame and emotional damage of Sexting.

Note: The Transform section is meant for the students to read on their own, as this is our advice to them directly. Present this as an in-class reading or a take-home reading assignment, then come back as a class and introduce the Topic For Discussion. For younger students, educators might want to translate some of these concepts.

For The Student: The Damage Is Done, How To Cope

Though most of the targets of Sexting are girls, boys who have girlfriends, sisters or gal pals should read this section to know how it feels. So, how does a girl "gain her power back" once she's given it away through Sexting photos? Martial Arts expert and bullying counselor Chuck Nguyen says facing the fear is the key to getting through this.

The excitement, thrill, and need for attention/affection through Sexting quickly can turn into fear and humiliation. This is especially true if the photos are misused by someone you trusted. Nothing can be more painful and damaging, to girls in particular, than being portrayed as **promiscuous**. In our double-standard society, boys are expected and allowed to be sexually aggressive with Sexting photos, but girls, put in the same position, are socially rejected for the same behaviors. How you cope after being a target of Sexting takes much personal power, **resiliency**, and a willingness to end the secret and face your actions. It's normal to feel embarrassed about taking those photos as well as fearing what your parents and friends will think, but Sexting has a way of going instantly **viral**, and most likely your parents and friends will find out from someone else. Tell yourself that this was a mistake—you just didn't realize how big. Own up to it. Go to your parents first and let them know what you did. Tell them, "I made a mistake and I need you to help me, not be angry with me. I'm already upset with myself. This is serious and I need your support to get through this."

Facing the Fear

The other side of fear comes from being exposed online and within multiple cell phone networks. No doubt you are worried how everyone at school might react once they find out. In Chuck's experience with teaching martial arts, fear comes from *not knowing the outcome . . .* and *envisioning the worst*. But to face fear after a catastrophic and humiliating event is an important step toward healing.

One of the first steps in facing the fear is figuring out where the threat is. In Sexting, pictures of yourself won't physically harm you. However, further emotional and social damage can continue if you choose *to do nothing* and allow the Sexting photos to go viral. In other words, the threat will continue to harm you unless you find the courage to do something about it and halt the transmission of the photos.

Finding Allies

Now is the time to talk with people who care about you. Who will unconditionally be friends and allies through the hurt and trauma? Chuck advises gathering a network of safe, supportive friends, family, trusted teachers, school counselors, and other allies who will help you through the aftermath of this situation with dignity.

Examine Your Motivations

Once you have people to support you, start to really think about what you wanted or needed from taking and sending those photos. This is the time to "soul search" and examine your own motivations and what social pressures factored in (if any) to prevent these same patterns of behavior from happening again the next time or with the next relationship. Ask yourself, "Do I want attention, acceptance, or am I wanting to cause some type of reaction?" Then consider what the recipient of the photo wanted too. "What was he or she trying to gain from asking me for my photos?" Boys and girls also need to examine the level of trust in the relationship itself. They both need to envision how they would handle it if the other person broke the pact of privacy by distributing a private sexualized photo. It's important to have this discussion *before it happens, not after.* If a person does not have the courage to say "no" to sending nude photos to a girlfriend/boyfriend for fear of being rejected, this is not a relationship that is healthy or good for either partner.

Forgive Yourself

Lastly, you need to forgive yourself. You are not an adult yet—you are a teenager, still growing up, still figuring out what are the good and bad choices in life. Have compassion for yourself and work on your personal **integrity** to not give in to anything you are uncomfortable with. Being a human means that we are sometimes vulnerable and make mistakes when we are confused about who we are and who we want to be. Know who you are and what you stand for and *do not give in* to what others might think of you based on their misinterpretation. Learn from your mistakes and make self-confident choices next time. This means finding ways to build up your self-esteem that are completely removed from your looks, body, or sexuality. If you can grow and learn from painful mistakes, it not only makes you stronger and more resilient, but you'll see there are other, healthier ways to express **intimacy** and affection in future relationships.

"I think one of the biggest ways to overcome any trial in life, to heal from any kind of experience, is by helping those around you, because by lifting those around you up, you end up lifting yourself up as well."[117]
—Elizabeth Smart

VOCAB WORDS

Integrity: Sticking to moral and ethical principles; soundness of moral character; honesty.

Intimacy: A close, familiar, and usually affectionate or loving personal relationship with another person.

Promiscuous: Having casual sexual relations frequently with different partners; lacking standards or being indiscriminate in the choice of sexual partners.

Resiliency: The ability to spring back from and successfully adapt to adversity.

Viral: When used as a computer term, this refers to a reoccurring practice or pattern of Internet use that moves from person to person.

Sexting Handouts Prevent: Group Activity
Collaborative Negotiation

Split your class into two groups, one representing Aaliyah and the other representing Lavon (it doesn't necessarily have to be along the same gender lines). This is a Collaborative Negotiation between Aaliyah and Lavon. Ask each group to imagine the two of them are able to talk to each other about what they both really want/need without involving either a sexual exchange or a Sexting photo. Expect a certain degree of discomfort and giggling around this exercise, but let your students know this is real-life practice on fostering effective communication. Ask each group to work through this list and provide answers from both of their perspectives.

Collaborative Negotiation	Aaliyah	Lavon
Agree to negotiate Are they both mature to see each other's point of view?	Yes No	Yes No
Gather points of view What do they both want or really need that has nothing to do with sex or a photo?		
Find common interests What are other common interests boys and girls have in a relationship apart from sex?		
Create win-win options List possible solutions for Aaliyah and Lavon to both get what they want without Sexting. List at least three possibly solutions each.	1. 2. 3.	1. 2. 3.
Evaluate options Now look at that list above. Which possible solutions are the most fair to both Aaliyah and Lavon?		
Formalize the agreement. Was your group able to come up with enough solutions to sign a Memorandum of Understanding? If not, why not?	Yes No	Yes No

Sample Memorandum of Understanding

This Memorandum of Understanding has been simplified for the purposes of creating an easy-to-understand template. Though the structure of this pact may seem overly formal in a real relationship, treat it as an exercise. Students may use this template when making other agreements or a "Friend Pact" around dissemination of photos.

THIS AGREEMENT is by and between

_____ (Name of Student #1) and

_____ (Name of Student #2)

for the purpose of finding a better alternative to Sexting.

The Parties agree as follows:

1.   _____ (Name of student #1) agrees to:
     1. (list a fair possible alternative to Sexting that works for Student #2)

     2. (list another fair possible alternative to Sexting that works for Student #2)

2.   _____ (Name of student #2) agrees to:
     1. (list a fair possible alternative to Sexting that works for Student #1)

     2. (list another fair possible alternative to Sexting that works for Student #1)

3.   This Agreement shall be effective from _____(date) to _____(date).

4.   This Agreement can only be modified by written consent of both Parties.

5.   This Agreement constitutes the entire Agreement between the Parties even if the friendship or the relationship ends.

Signatures

Student #1_____   Student #2_____

  Date: _____   Date: _____

Combat: Group Activity
Threat Level Assessments

Low-Risk

You're over the age of eighteen and take a sexy (but not nude) photo of yourself then send it to your boyfriend, who is also eighteen or older. He does the same. The photos have not been seen or distributed to anyone else yet, but you have reasons to think they might soon. What do you do?

_____

_____

_____

_____

_____

_____

_____

Guarded Risk

You are under the age of eighteen and send a semi-nude photo (face showing) to someone also under eighteen. The image is only a day old but has been sent around to two or three friends. So far, no evidence of the photos has been found online. However, someone's mom has found it and now has contacted your parents. What do you do?

_____

_____

_____

_____

_____

_____

Elevated Risk

You are under the age of eighteen and have taken semi-nude photos of yourself (face showing) and sent it by cell phone to someone over eighteen who has uploaded it to a social networking site or a website. What do you do?

_____

_____

_____

_____

_____

_____

_____

High-Risk

You are under the age of eighteen and have taken explicit nude photos of yourself (some with face visible) with your cell phone but haven't sent them to anyone. Someone you don't know has retrieved them from your cell phone and has circulated them to multiple recipients. A public website/profile/blog is now featuring the photos online. What do you do?

_____

_____

_____

_____

_____

_____

Video Tactics: Videojacking

Videojacking:

A hybrid word combining videotaping with hijacking, as in to steal, swindle, or subject the target to extortion.

This tactic refers to a bully who videotapes the target on a cell phone, digital camera, or camcorder, or else finds existing footage and uploads potentially embarrassing or denigrating video online to popular video-sharing sites like YouTube without the express permission or knowledge of the target.

Getting Started

Lesson Rundown Students are introduced to the concept of Videojacking in which the bully videotapes a target without his knowledge and uploads the video to a popular video-sharing website for the purpose of humiliation and ridicule.

Objective Students will be able to:

- understand how a video can be used against a target and go "viral" or turn into a "meme";
- assess how to use social skills and tech defense to prevent being caught on videotape;
- empathize with the suffering a target endures in the guise of public entertainment;
- determine when and how to take a digital stand in the aftermath of a Videojacking incident.

Time Needed: The Understand, Combat, and Transform sections are structured to be conducted within a typical classroom requiring 30-40 minutes of lesson time. The Prevent sections may require 30-60 minutes as they go more in-depth and may prompt more conversation. Total estimated time for the Videojacking Unit is 2–3 hours and will vary in an after-school or workshop environment.

Teacher Prep Review any group or individual activities ahead of time for materials needed to maximize in-class time.

Equipment/ Supplies Needed Computers with Internet access can be used for high-tech activities. Otherwise, paper and writing materials can be used for low-tech activities.

Vocab Words Defined at the end of this section.

Handouts *Threat Level Assessments*

For The Educator

Tactic Overview

We'll discuss how and why certain videos get singled out to go "viral" and the popular culture behind it. Our goal is to teach educators how Videojacking is done, who participates, and ways to help students proactively avoid falling victim to this type of tactic.

How Videojacking Happens: More than any other type of online content, video provides an instant entertainment angle. Starting in the mid-2000s, home videos and other creative video content exploded across the Internet. People now watch two billion videos a day on YouTube, the leading video-sharing service worldwide, and upload hundreds of thousands of videos daily.[118] Although few teenagers will find themselves under intense national scrutiny because of a homemade uploaded video, two cautionary tales regarding Videojacking explain how and why a seemingly innocent video can turn into worldwide Internet entertainment. The following true stories involve "The Star Wars Kid" and Aleksey Vayner, both of whom found themselves unwitting jokes and objects of ridicule on video-sharing sites.

The most popular viral video of all time still circulates around the Internet featuring a Canadian high school student named Ghyslain Raza, who, in 2002, videotaped himself playing with lightsabers as he acted out a scene from *Star Wars*. Three classmates found the video and uploaded it to the Internet without his permission. Dubbed *The Star Wars Kid* by the Internet community and the media, Raza's video got more than a billion hits online. The incessant attention, harassment, and ridicule took a heavy toll on the bewildered teenager, who'd never asked for this kind of attention. Diagnosed with depression, he dropped out of his Quebec high school and had to take time off from school to seek psychiatric care. Raza and his parents ended up suing the families of the three classmates who leaked the video. According to the lawsuit, which resulted in a settlement, "Ghyslain had to endure, and still endures today, harassment and derision from his high-school mates and the public at large."[119]

Like Raza, Aleksey Vayner became famous against his will. In his case, he created an Internet résumé video to show to potential employers, but the video leaked out to the public. Vayner didn't realize how his video might have appeared outside its intended audience. What seemed funny to others soon spiraled out of control. Inexplicably, Vayner received intense online harassment as well as death threats for simply having uploaded what he considered a serious video résumé.[120]

With the popularity of video-sharing sites, short video clips featuring teens doing silly things, beating each other up, mocking other students, and other forms of "creativity" are being uploaded every day. Depending on the circumstances, a video can immediately go **viral**, which means getting an excessive number of hits—and/or become a **meme** and mutate (fostering imitations called **mashups**) as a cultural form of entertainment.

Secret Videotaping

It is bad enough when a video is uploaded revealing embarrassing or foolish footage for all the world to see, but when a bully secretly videotapes a target without his knowledge, (as in the case of two Rutgers university students who used a hidden web cam to "**out**" an eighteen-year-old boy named Tyler Clementi in their dorm), the consequences can be disastrous. Four days after the videotaping incident received nationwide attention, Clementi committed suicide, something the students in his residence hall likely never contemplated when they secretly turned on the web cam.[121]

Though horrific repercussions like these may have been compounded with other issues affecting Clementi's psychological state, it is still imperative to teach students **empathy** and **foreseeable consequences** to their behavior. Even if the audience viewing the Videojacked video is comprised of four to five people as opposed to millions, the target still can suffer humiliation on a scale which can and does contribute to severe depression, loss of will, and, in some cases, even suicide.

Five Most Popular Video-Sharing Sites[122]

- **YouTube**
- **Vimeo**
- **Metacafe**
- **Hulu**
- **Veoh**

Scenario
Kahn's Story

Print the below story and hand out to the students. For more interactivity, assign someone to read it to the entire class.

Unkind Rewind

Kahn, a 9th grader, set up the video camcorder in his bedroom and switched on the controls to begin recording. He stared at the camera for a moment and cleared his throat. "Here goes," he said. He began to sing a Michael Jackson ballad, "Never Can Say Goodbye." He'd been a big fan of Jorge Nunez, an American Idol contestant from Puerto Rico, and began to try to imitate his version of the song. Kahn ignored how off-pitch his voice was; after all, he was just practicing. As he got more into the song, he closed his eyes and swayed a little. The higher the pitch of the song, the more his voice began cracking. He braved on, continuing to get through the song, despite how screechy he sounded. At one point in the song, he forgot the lyrics and made up some nonsense words. Finally, when the song concluded, he stared at the camera and said somberly, "Thank you, American Idol."

A few weeks later, his father used the camcorder to film Kahn's oldest sister, Soni, at her dance recital. Soni brought the tape over to her best friend Kelsey's house so they could watch it, but they forgot all about it and Soni forgot to take it home. Kelsey's brother, Derek, was the one to discover the DV tape sitting in the video camera, which was hooked up to their giant TV. His friends were over that day and as they turned on the TV, the screen fuzzed out for a moment. Next, appeared Kahn, doing his nervous, screechy rendition of "Never Can Say Goodbye." Derek and his friends fell over laughing. "Oh, this is *so* going on YouTube!" Derek said, scooping up the tape.

Within days, Kahn's painfully awkward performance sparked a flurry of 80,000 hits online. Soon, the video spiraled into YouTube notoriety and jumped to CNN's web page. From there, Kahn's life became nonstop misery. Every single day at school, people yelled "fag" in the hallways at lunch and even told him to go back to "his own country." The more viral the video became, the more he became harassed at school, out in public, through email, and even prank calls. He had no idea how the video got online and who was behind it. And why were they connecting that video with being gay? He couldn't even walk around his own town without strangers pointing and laughing at him. His parents had no idea how to stop it.

Within a month, the video spawned neatly four million hits on YouTube, producing multiple mashups and **parodies** online. Trying to get the video down proved futile, as more versions of it were uploaded by strangers every day. When three months had passed and the video did not go away—Kahn dropped out of school. It had become a constant torment to him, being shoved into lockers, people laughing at him the moment he entered the room, calling names out wherever he went. It was impossible to forget the video clip when the rest of the world seemed endlessly fascinated by it. He felt that he would never live this down. The final straw came one day when he flipped on one of his favorite animated sitcoms known for its silly and sarcastic humor. There, right in the middle of the show, was a character who looked exactly like him, singing that Michael Jackson song, "Never Can Say Goodbye." It had come down to the whole world being against him. So depressed he could barely get up, Kahn switched off the TV. It took several years of counseling and support from many strangers who contacted him, for Kahn to eventually come out of his depression and begin to live a normal life again.

Step I: Understand

Objective	Students will be able to:

- differentiate between what is entertaining and what is cruel by putting themselves in the target's shoes;
- understand the legal consequences of Videojacking;
- understand how "passive supporters" and followers contribute to the bullying aspect of this tactic.

Time Needed	55 minutes.
Teacher Prep	Copy handouts of the Scenario for the class or display through a wall projector and have students vocalize the roles of the characters.
Equipment/ Supplies Needed	Copier. Computers with Internet access (high-tech) or paper and pencils (low-tech).
Vocab Words	Defined at the end of this section.

Overview

Start with the Topic for Discussion to get students warmed up. Gradually move on to show them the various roles people play in this particular tactic.

Establish Group Guidelines	See the guidelines in **Appendix C** in order to get the most out of your group discussions in class.
Topic for Discussion	Ask students to examine why a moment in time captured by video can be more embarrassing than just if it happened unrecorded?
Define Tactic	There are multiple ways one's video can be hijacked. Define the tactic and ask if anyone has ever been a target of being videotaped without permission.
For The Student: A Broader Perspective	Online conflict isn't always clear-cut. Once you've gotten through the Topic For Discussion, go over the roles of each participant in the scenario with your class. We've provided multiple perspectives to help students gain insight.

From The Bully's Perspective: First, let's consider why bullies love reputation-smearing. *Newsweek* writer Neal Gabler blames our **Tabloid Culture** as the "great new art form of the twenty-first century." To understand why so many people are addicted to celebrity news, reality shows, and drama, Gabler explains that celebrities are 'human entertainments'—not people who exist to be publicized, but people whose lives seem to exist to provide us with ongoing amusement."[123] Teenagers today have been raised on incessant media, following the ups and downs, triumphs and humiliations of celebrities in "Tabloid Culture" on a daily basis as a way to keep amused, entertained, and to pass judgment. Now, think about how much teen drama exists in high school hallways and in digital "hallways." Smearing someone's reputation is just another way to stay hooked on the entertainment of drama, to provide others with ongoing amusement.

The bullies in this case are clearly Derek and his friends, who uploaded the video as a joke without Kahn's knowledge. Neither Derek nor his friends actually even knew Kahn and had no reason to dislike him. They wouldn't have even *considered* themselves bullies, particularly because Kahn filmed the video himself. Derek and his friends were just uploading what they thought was a hilarious video. Even they couldn't have known that it would spin so out of control or that the school would eventually try to suspend them for their actions. This is a typical example of bullies not thinking about how their actions might harm others, only to see it go horribly wrong. Kahn suffered so much abuse, he chose to drop out of school and had to undergo therapy. As a result, Kahn's parents eventually took legal action against Derek, his family and his friends' families. Who would have ever imagined uploading a video could cause this much damage?

From The Target's Perspective: From the start, Kahn was bewildered that anyone would have bothered to upload a video of him singing. He didn't know the bullies and they clearly had nothing against him. He was careless with the video footage, not aware that it could possibly be seen as "funny" to someone else or that anyone would actually do anything with it. As a result, he found himself inexplicably in the center of a pop culture phenomenon that grew bigger than anything he or the bullies could control. The worst thing about that video capturing him in that awkward way is that no one could let it go. A couple of fleeting moments were forever preserved on the Internet, giving the viewer the mistaken impression that Kahn *always* behaved like a fool, instead of having it be just one isolated moment in digital history.

The humiliating video wasn't the only harm done. Other bullies at his school were encouraged by the video incident to call him a "fag," along with other hateful statements about his race and background. In a 2011 MTV/AP Study, students admitted that they often see discriminatory language being used against others such as "slut," "That's so gay," "fag," and "retard" ranking among the most commonly used discriminatory words or phrase in cyberbullying. They know it to be wrong; yet they admit they're emboldened to say these slurs online they would never say to a person's face.[124] Students need to step outside their belief systems to realize how indescribably *painful* it is for anyone to deal with harassment, threats, and violence directed at him or her on a daily basis based on the perception of being different. This includes: **homophobic bullying**, **racial bullying,** and being bullied because of one's religion or disability. In Kahn's situation he was getting bullied for the video, for being Indian, and for being perceived as gay. Not everyone believes in the same values, but it's wrong to abuse and persecute *anyone* you perceive to be different. At the root of it all, having empathy for others is essential for teenagers in the Digital Age.

From The Bystanders' Perspective: The students at Kahn's school who watched the video were both passive supporters as well as followers, especially when the bullying jumped offline and Kahn was verbally taunted and physically assaulted at school. Because of the viral nature of the Internet and all the media attention, the millions of people who watched the video and commented became followers just by participating—including those who made imitations and mashups for fun. What about the late night talk show host who made fun of Kahn? Or the parody from the animated sitcom? Consider that the damage done by adults and the media in this case was arguably so much more destructive than what the bullies did by uploading the video.

From The Allies' Perspective: Even though bystanders made his life worse, Kahn's video also elicited the support of thousands of allies who tried to help him. Many who viewed the video sent emails of support to Kahn and wrote sympathetic columns and blogs about him. Many adults and students who'd witnessed what he'd gone through offered him **sympathy** and stories of dumb things they'd done that had gotten captured on video camera. It was a very painful time for him during those years, but the more Kahn received support from strangers and friends alike, the more it helped him move beyond this horrible experience. He grew stronger, knowing that this one video moment in time would not define who he was going to grow up to be.

Some people will argue that comments, imitations, and mashups are free speech, and the video and its parodies were a natural progression of content sharing. Internet forums on this subject are predictably divided and shrill. We contend it is wrong to defame and destroy a teenager's self worth and mental stability in the name of creativity and free speech. It will be interesting to see how everyone else in your class feels when it crosses the line of entertainment.

Group Activity

High-tech: Ask the students to Google Ghyslain Raza, "The Star Wars Kid" and Aleksey Vayner, and watch the videos online as small groups. If they haven't seen these two viral videos before, expect that their reactions may lack empathy at first. Then allow them to read the comments that people have made about the videos (you might want to preview for language beforehand). The objective is to look at these videos through the lens of our cultural fascination with ridiculing others. Ask each of your students to put themselves in the targets' shoes by writing in their own words supportive statements to Ghyslain Raza or Aleksey Vayner as if they were still kids in your students' own school. Note: we've used this technique in workshops and it helps kids cultivate their roles as allies to "**post play**" a scenario in which they can write their support to the targets as if it is happening in the present.

Low-tech: It's really best to be able to have students watch this video, as it is much harder to explain it than see it. If your class doesn't have access to the Internet, then print out some negative comments you find on Ghyslain Raza or Aleksey Vayner. Ask your students to analyze the reasons why people write mean and negative things about someone they don't know. On 3 x 5 index cards, ask each of your students to put themselves in the targets' shoes by writing supportive statements to Ghyslain Raza or Aleksey Vayner as if they were still kids in your students' own school.

Teacher Takeaway Tip

Remember, not everyone in class will have empathy for the targets of this particular tactic; some will be derisive, so expect this. The point we will continue to emphasize throughout this chapter is to encourage students to generate empathy and proactive skills for future targets of this tactic.

VOCAB WORDS

Empathy: The ability to understand and share the feelings of another.

Foreseeable Consequences: Consequences to one's actions that can be predicted or anticipated before the action occurs.

Homophobic Bullying: Harassment directed toward gay/ lesbian/ bisexual/ transgender (GBLT) teens.

Mashup: A song or composition created by blending two or more pre-recorded songs, usually by overlaying the vocal track of one song seamlessly over the instrumental track of another.

Meme: An idea, behavior, style, or usage that spreads from person to person within a culture.

Out: A common term for publicizing that someone is gay without their consent and/or knowledge.

Parody: A work created to mock, comment on, or poke fun at an original work.

Post-Play: In "role-playing" this means analyzing what happened in the game (or scenario) after it happens, to know what to do in the event of a similar situation next time.

Racial Bullying: Harassment directed toward a student of one color by a student or students of a predominantly different color in the school.

Sympathy: Feelings of pity and sorrow for someone else's misfortune.

Tabloid Culture: Contemporary mainstream media culture that elevates tabloid newscasts, reality TV, and celebrity news into a twenty-first century "art form."

Viral: When used as a computer term, this refers to a reoccurring practice or pattern of Internet use that moves from person to person.

Step II: Prevent

Objective

Students will be able to:

- introduce the concept of empathy and compassion for others;
- practice positive reactions the next time one encounters this tactic;
- protect themselves with behavioral and technological strategies to prevent being the target of a Videojacking.

Time Needed

30-60 minutes.

Teacher Prep

You will need pieces of blank paper and pencils for each student. A printer is needed to print out transcripts.

Equipment/ Supplies Needed

A computer lab and printer would be beneficial for this section, but the individual and group activity can both be done in low-tech classrooms with paper and pencils.

Vocab Words

Defined at the end of this section.

For The Educator: Conflict Resolution Concepts

Now that the students have identified the roles of bullies, targets, and bystanders, it is time to "post-play" the opening scenario to get them to understand how to put themselves in another's shoes. In this section we will work with **Empathy Skills**.

Some teenagers may be more compassionate or empathetic, whether they were raised that way or have an innate ability to respond in that manner, while others have not been taught to develop these skills. Teacher/author David A. Levine developed an empathy-building exercise below called the **Event Empathy Action** (EEA). The EEA is a three-step advanced listening approach that teaches students how to respond to others with empathy.[125]

Individual Activity   The following activity works best in a low-tech classroom and doesn't necessarily have to be shared with the rest of the class. Ask students to think about someone they witnessed get humiliated in some way by writing down three **Event Empathy Action** questions. Pretend that the incident has just recently happened.

1. What happened? (Identify the event)
2. How is that person feeling? (Imagine the other person's feelings)
3. What will I do? (Decide on a specific action)

Students can use different names or just the first letter of the target's name to preserve anonymity if they wish.

Self-Defense   On the board, write down two columns: **Behavior** and **Tech Defense**. Ask your class to volunteer their own suggestions to prevent being the target of a Videojacking and follow up by presenting the strategies below.

Behavior

- **Pays To Be Paranoid**: All of your videos should pass the "Would I Be Embarrassed If This Video Got Out?" test. Never take or send digital footage of yourself or allow others to take video that is embarrassing, inappropriate, overly sexualized . . . and sadly, it has to be said, even innocently silly. Always remember in this technological age, video in the wrong hands can change the content of the video's meaning instantly, and negatively damage your reputation for years.

- **Friend Pact**: Ask your friends to make a **"friend pact"** that no one will ever upload another's video without permission. Use Chapter Five's Memorandum of Understanding as a template. Tell your friends they should *always* ask you before uploading any videos of you and that you *never* give permission to post videos that are negative or compromising.

- **Embarrassing . . . Or Not?**: Each teen's comfort with a certain amount of Internet exposure is an individual preference. In the age of reality TV and Internet shows, some kids actually delight in doing something silly or foolish so that they can claim their YouTube fame as a badge of honor. That goes back to William Glasser's **Need For Power**—fulfilled by achieving, accomplishing, and being recognized and respected. Others feel safe being themselves in front of close friends, but would be horrified if anyone outside their circle saw the footage. Still, others can't stand the idea of being videotaped at all. Consider that any video you upload yourself now may be perceived negatively when your future employer or new relationship finds it online when you're older.

Tech Defense

Here are some YouTube tips listed on its own site to prevent being a target of cyberbullying and harassment.

- **Set To Private**: Set all of your video-sharing accounts to private. Never post personal information on your profile, such as the town you live in, where you go to school, your full name, or your home address. If a video contains personal information without your consent, such as your image, name, voice, home address, telephone number, national identification number, or financial records, please contact YouTube through their Privacy Removal Process.[126]

- **Block Users And Comments**: You can block users from making comments on your own videos or sending you messages by going to their profiles and clicking the "**Block User**" button in the "Connect with" box. You also have control over blocking users' comments as well.[127]

- **Make A Video Pact**: Encourage your friends who've uploaded a video to block or monitor comments. You can turn comment voting off for each video. Do this when you upload a video by clicking the "Sharing Options" window and choosing an option next to "Comment Voting."[128]

- **Harassment Help**: If someone has crossed the line from making rude comments to tricking you, harassing you, spreading lies and rumors about you, or filming you without your consent, consult YouTube's **Help and Safety Tool**, which helps you remove content on your own, blocks other users, and if appropriate, reports the content to the YouTube Team.[129]

Group Activity   Split the class into three groups. Ask each group to research a well-known target of cyberbullying in the news and on the Internet. Then each group may answer each of the **Event Empathy Questions** below, allowing enough time to discuss their responses with one another while someone in the group takes notes. Allow each group to present to the rest of the class the background and situation of the cyberbullying target they chose and their answers to the Event Empathy Action questions.

Ask someone in the class to volunteer to write these suggestions down on the blackboard or flip chart.

1: What happened? (Identify the target and what happened to him or her.)
2: How is he or she feeling? (Describe the possible feelings the target has felt.)
3: What will I do? (Act as though you had the power to help the target while it was happening. What would your group do to help him or her?)

VOCAB WORDS

Block User: To stop someone from accessing your online account.

Empathy Skills: Skills you develop to share the sadness or happiness of another person or a creature and ability to have compassion for them.

Event Empathy Action: A three-step advanced listening approach that teaches students how to respond to others empathically.

Friend Pact: A formal agreement made and signed by two or more friends.

Help and Safety Tool: YouTube's Help Center for cyberbullying and harassment which helps you remove content on your own, blocks other users, and if appropriate, reports to the YouTube Team.

Need for Power: William Glasser's definition pertaining to one of the five psychological human needs: to be in control of one's own social and personal power.

Step III: Combat

Objective	Students will be able to:

- identify low-to high-risk online situations;
- assess possible solutions to remedy conflict without resorting to revenge;
- practice making thoughtful, deliberate choices on how to react to the threat.

Time Needed   30 minutes.

Teacher Prep   Read any section ahead of class time labeled "For the Educator." Make a copy each of the Threat Level Assessments to hand out to four small groups.

Equipment/   Copier for handouts and paper and pencils for students.
Supplies Needed

Vocab Words   Defined at the end of this section.

In the following section we use our own version of the US Department of Defense's concept of "Threat Levels" when providing students action steps to take.

Note: the advice in this section does not purport to be legal advice. We have consulted with cyberbullying experts to help parents and students know what to do in a Videojacking situation.

Immediate Steps To Take
First Step: Identify The Problem

In this section, we reference YouTube because it is the largest video-sharing site and because they have practical advice on how to combat video violations. Flag the video and notify the video-sharing site right away through their Help and Safety Tool. Again, this is a YouTube term, and it might be called something else if you are dealing with another video-sharing website. Include a carefully worded statement why you thought the video was abusive, offensive, or harassing, etc. Provide as many relevant details (who, what, where, when), including who owns the video footage, and remember to save this as evidence in a separate document, such as the **Scene Survey (Appendix B)**.

Automatic Violation Checklist: To help you identify the harassing issue, the following are automatic violations of YouTube's Community Guidelines and could cause the video to be removed and/or the poster to be banned.

- *Copyright infringement:* Any portion of video or audio posted without the permission of the original owner of that content.
- *Children under eighteen in the video:* Video-sharing sites are particularly sensitive to anything that violates a child's rights.
- *Identifying information:* The video or its comments section contains personal info about you, such as your name, phone number, email, and where you live.
- *Impersonation:* The video attempts to impersonate you by using a similar username or posing as you [See Chapter Three: Imposter Profile].
- *Inappropriate content:* The video contains footage of you doing something illegal, such as underage drinking, drugs, or anything else against the law.
- *Deliberate humiliation and/or harassment:* If the video shows you being physically hurt, attacked, or humiliated, or someone is exhibiting predatory behavior such as stalking, threats, harassment, or other intimidation, report it. Also important: if the perpetrator tries to incite others to harass you or violate the Terms of Use, he or she can be permanently banned.
- *Sexually explicit content:* If the video shows you in your underwear or unclothed in

any way [See Chapter Five: Sexting]. The perpetrator could also be charged with trafficking child pornography.[130]

Second Step: Fill out Scene Survey and Keep Evidence

Before we get into the Threat Level Assessment, take a **Scene Survey** (**Appendix B**) to gather as many facts, dates, and evidence as possible. If the situation escalates, this starts the fact-based paper trail that parents, school administrators, video-sharing sites, and law enforcement will need to see from the beginning.

Threat Level Assessment

In this section, the group activity comes before the lesson. This allows students to "pre-play" how they might react to each escalating situation. *Educators will need to make copies of the four Threat Assessments at the end of this chapter before the group activity can begin.*

Group Activity   Split the class into four small groups and ask them to retreat to each corner of the room. Assign each group a hypothetical situation ranging from Low-Risk to High-Risk (handouts found at the end of this chapter). Appoint a group leader to read the Threat Assessment on each handout to the group, and give each group a chance to write down their solutions to each hypothetical situation. After each group is done, ask the group leader (starting with Low-Risk) to read the group's suggestions out loud to the class. Educators can provide the correct answer from the "What To Do" guide below for each Threat Level.

1. **Low-Risk**: You come across a public video on a friend's social networking site that shows you in a mildly embarrassing or silly situation and you didn't want anyone but your friends to see it.

    Frequency: It happens once, but not many people have seen it or have commented on it.

What To Do: If a friend uploaded it, resolve this by calmly and politely requesting that he or she remove the video because it makes you uncomfortable. Most likely your friend didn't realize how it would affect you, so don't assume initially that the person is trying to be a bully. Give your friend a chance to take the video down and don't make any threats. However, if after you've reasonably requested the removal of the video and your friend refuses or fails to do so, record the date of your conversation and as much detail as you can remember. This is the start of your evidence paper trail. Start with the website hosting the video; it should have complaint forms you can fill out. Immediately flag the video and file a complaint with the video-sharing site citing the reason as "deliberate humiliation and harassment," along with your evidence paper trail.

2. **Guarded Risk**: You come across a video of yourself that reveals you doing something not just embarrassing, but could get you in trouble with adults/parents/ school administrators.

   Frequency: It happens once, but the video is getting a lot of hits. People are starting to talk about it at school.

   What To Do: Speak to the person who uploaded it and firmly but politely request that he or she remove the video immediately. Explain that this isn't just personal, but it's now putting you at risk. Follow the steps in Low-Risk. Again flag the video and fill out a complaint form with the video-sharing site, citing the reason as "deliberate humiliation and harassment," along with your evidence paper trail. Do not put out a campaign to ask people to stop viewing it, as it will just cause more people to find it. If you are in a situation where the person deliberately uploaded the video to harm your reputation, tell your parents or a trusted adult now, rather than wait and see if you can "fix" this yourself. The more the video goes viral, the more adults will find out. Even if video was shot and/or posted off school grounds, the school administration may get involved, especially if drugs, alcohol, or illegal behavior is present in the video. The best way to manage your reputation at this point is to come clean, admit your mistakes, and allow the adults to handle the video takedown process.

3. **Elevated Risk**: You come across a video of yourself on a video-sharing site or a **parody** video of you that makes reference to threatening or killing you, or posts

hate speech about your race, sexual orientation, gender, or posts personal information designed to encourage others to harass, stalk, or threaten you.

Frequency: The video has not been removed and continues to get lots of hits and comments.

What To Do: Immediately show the video to your parents, school administrators, and law enforcement. There are serious legal consequences for anyone making real-life threats using video as the platform. If the video-sharing site is set to private, get help from the police or the video-sharing provider to remove it. If you are getting nowhere with these steps, have a friend join the private group and capture the offending video by going to KeepVid (http://.keepvid.com) or a similar site to download and save any video from YouTube, DailyMotion, Metacafe, iFilm, and more. The purpose is to save anything on DVD to be able to show police and/or attorneys. The only exception to this advice is if the video contains underage nudity, in which case, *do not download or save anything* and follow the advice in the Threat Level Assessments of the "Sexting" chapter. Remember to keep a **Scene Survey (Appendix B)** on all dates this occurs.

4. **High-Risk**: Someone has uploaded a video of you without your knowledge or consent. The video becomes a **meme** and goes viral by getting hundreds of thousands of hits every day. It seems every area of your life has been invaded by this video from home to school to your community, both online and off.

Frequency: The video has not been removed, has gone viral, and continues to get an extremely large number of hits and comments.

What To Do: Follow all the advice in the previous three levels. At this point, consider consulting with a cyber crime attorney with police reports and all of your saved evidence. If someone sets out to commit Intentional/Negligent Infliction of Emotional Distress, that person (or people) can be sued for damages. If the bullying continues to persist at school because of this video (even if the video wasn't posted on school grounds), the school administration has a legal responsibility to protect a student from harassment. Eventually, like all memes, people get tired and move on to the next thing. You will need some help in transforming this experience, so call on your friends, family, and other support systems to help you, and consult our Transform section below.

Topic For Discussion   Now that everyone has had a chance to see how a Videojacking incident works, ask your students what they are going to do the next time they are at a party and someone starts taking video of them that makes them uncomfortable. How would they handle this legally and ethically in order to make sure no video ends up online?

VOCAB WORDS

Meme: An idea, behavior, style, or usage that spreads from person to person within a culture.

Parody: A work created to mock, comment on, or poke fun at an original work.

Scene Survey: A practical, shorthand system to get all the facts about a cyberbullying incident before making a plan or decision. This can be found in **Appendix B**.

Step IV: Transform

Objective

Students will be able to:

- recognize the most vulnerable and empathize with those who might be harassed;
- practice making thoughtful, deliberate choices on how to cope throughout a viral video ordeal;
- "pre-play" how they would deal with being targets of a Videojacking if it happened to them.

Time Needed

30 minutes.

Teacher Prep

Allow students to read this section by themselves. For younger students, translate the concepts for better understanding.

Equipment/ Supplies Needed

Paper and pencils for students to take notes during Topic for Discussion.

Vocab Words

Defined at the end of this section.

Teacher Tip

This section is best absorbed if read first by the educator and used as a basis for a Topic For Discussion at the end.

Note: The Transform section is meant for the students to read on their own, as this is our advice to them directly. Present this as an in-class reading or a take-home reading assignment, and then come back as a class and introduce the Topic For Discussion. For younger students, educators might want to translate some of these concepts.

For The Student: The Damage Is Done, How To Cope

One of the biggest fears a victimized person has is that that the initial bullying will go on and on, like some kind of nightmare that won't end. The strategies presented here are ways of not just surviving the initial bullying, but putting a stop to the endlessness of it.

Anyone can appreciate the anger, rage, and ultimately hopelessness that someone experiences after being badly mistreated like this. Most targets of a Videojacking are devastated because they can't understand why other students would purposely humiliate them so publicly. Martial Arts expert and Bullying Counselor Chuck Nguyen tells us the way someone can cope and transform after being a target of a Videojacking tactic truly requires inner strength and character.

When To Play It Off

Chuck works with young people every day in high school after they are pushed, teased, and beaten verbally and physically. For students who are targeted, he uses the metaphor of a cat. If the student is lightly teased or harassed in a "Low-Risk" situation listed in the Combat section of this chapter, he encourages them to minimize the attention they bring to themselves and to "play" with the bullies to knock them off track. Imagine yourself as a cat playing with a much bigger dog. Instead of hissing and drawing the dog into a fight, imagine instead bobbing and weaving, signaling to the dog that you're playing and getting him to play back, to defuse the situation. A student can also borrow strategies from well-known comedians by being self-deprecating or making a joke about the video. Another strategy is to **parody** one's own video by adding creative effects or music to it and uploading it to his or her own social networking site. It might be a gamble, but taking control of one's own video and demonstrating you're able to laugh at yourself shows that you are **resilient** and not bothered by what others think of you.

When To Take A Stand

If the video is deliberately harmful and people are making nasty comments online and off, an entire other strategy needs to be used. Do not tell the bullies your feelings are hurt. In situations like these, bullies are encouraged by knowing they have gotten you to react with fear or distress. At this point, Chuck suggests you take a stand. Like a stressed and threatened cat, you need to stand up tall, draw your claws, and tell the bully to stop and back off.

How do you take a stand digitally? Confronting the bullies is difficult since there can be thousands of bystanders who take on the role of the bully by joining in on the comments (essentially keep the drama going for entertainment). One of the best online techniques to divert unwanted attention from distorted things people are saying about you is to put out a message that you can control and others can't, such as a website that allows no comment sections. Websites such as Snopes (www.snopes.com) and Truth or Fiction (www.truthorfiction.com) regularly separate facts from circulating rumors and can be used for a model of what you're trying to do. State the truth and the facts, including if the police are involved and nothing more. Don't engage in name-calling or get emotionally caught up in defending yourself. Most people look for the truth and know a manufactured drama when they see it for themselves, so when people can see "both" sides of the story on the target's own website, many will understand there is a human being behind all of this.

Dealing with Homophobic or Racial Bullying

When cyberbullying turns homophobic or racial, the target and sympathetic witnesses (allies) need to turn their rage about homosexual slurs and racial harassment into **social outrage**. Social outrage, in the form of activism, can happen in the classroom, school, community, and at a government level. Consider joining or starting an activist group or Civil Rights group with an adult at your school that your friends and fellow students can rally behind, making it known that people at your school don't tolerate the behaviors of online aggression, reputation bashing, and underhanded tactics through cyberbullying to anyone regardless of their race, gender, sexuality, religion, or disability.

Lean On Friends And Family

As always, this is the time when you need to turn to your close friends and family for support. It also helps to find other targeted kids who've been through similar cyberbullying situations so that you know you are not alone. YouTube has a group called "Cyber Bully Stoppers" (www.YouTube.com/group/CyberBullyStoppers). Another powerfully effective YouTube video series called the "It Gets Better Project" (www.youtube.com/user/itgetsbetterproject) helps teens transform a horrible bullying/cyberbullying experience with short videos from celebrities and public figures who've lived through bullying and have come away stronger from it.[131]

As mentioned earlier, Videojacking target Aleksey Vayner had been through a wrenching ordeal. Here's what he had to say about his whole experience: "Once you present any type of content to the wrong market, it's going to be misinterpreted . . . and taken out of context. When a viewer was looking at [my video] who has never seen me and doesn't know why it was created, the perception was that it was all me-focused . . . this arrogant jerk." Asked how he got through being made fun of incessantly, he recalls with a painful sigh, "I would say I hit rock bottom. There were a lot of components that hurt. One is . . . we're all affected by our peers and getting so much peer pressure and negative feedback, you start to question yourself. You start questioning your **core beliefs** and **convictions**, and that becomes a problem. As negative as the publicity was, it made me realize how incredibly powerful the Internet was. You take a step back and reflect on your core fundamental beliefs. I didn't kill a man. I wasn't driving drunk, I don't drink or smoke or do anything bad per say. *I created a video.* The best way I can judge myself and what happened . . . is that I didn't lose any core friendships."[132]

One last word about The Star Wars Kid—Ghyslain Raza. At the time of this printing, he was in the process of getting his law degree at McGill University in Montreal.[133]   And as we all know, in the real world, a law degree is a lot more powerful than a lightsaber. This is not only a triumph over the personal pain and humiliation he suffered as a teen, but it's a powerful message to those who have ever been set back by cyberbullying. Even when you think you're at rock bottom—it's temporary. What happened to you will not only make you stronger, it'll open your eyes to what other kids in your position have been through—and perhaps give you a reason to teach others to learn from your experience. People like Ghyslain Raza who've survived the worst cyberbullying possible now have a strength in character and dignity that their bullies will never have. And you, too, must continue being that powerful, ethical, compassionate, and kind person you have it in you to be.

The most beautiful people we have known are those who have known defeat, known suffering, known struggle, known loss, and have found their way out of the depths. These persons have an appreciation, sensitivity, and an understanding of life that fills them with compassion, gentleness, and a deep loving concern. Beautiful people do not just happen.

—Elizabeth Kubler Ross

VOCAB WORDS

Core beliefs: Beliefs that you hold deep inside that you know and trust to be true.

Conviction: A firmly held belief or opinion.

Parody: A work created to mock, comment on, or poke fun at an original work.

Resiliency: The power or ability to recover readily from illness, depression, adversity.

Social Outrage: A form of group activism to change the negative behaviors of a society.

Videojacking Handouts
Combat: Group Activity
Threat Level Assessment

Low-Risk

You come across a public video on a friend's social networking site that shows you in a mildly embarrassing or silly situation and you didn't want anyone but your friends to see it. What do you do?

_____

_____

_____

_____

_____

_____

_____

Guarded Risk

You come across a video of yourself that reveals you doing something not just embarrassing, but could get you in trouble with adults/parents/school administrators. What do you do?

_____

_____

_____

_____

_____

_____

_____

Elevated Risk

You come across a video of yourself on a video-sharing site or a "parody" video of you that makes reference to threatening or killing you, or posts hate speech about your race, sexual orientation, gender, or posts personal information designed to encourage others to harass, stalk, or threaten you. What do you do?

_____

_____

_____

_____

_____

_____

_____

_____

High-Risk

Someone has uploaded a video of you without your knowledge or consent. The video becomes a meme and goes viral, getting hundreds of thousands of hits every day. It seems every area of your life has been invaded by this video from home, to school, to your community, both online and off. There seems no end to it. What do you do?

_____

_____

_____

_____

_____

_____

_____

Final Class Project Idea

After going through two, three, or even all six of the cyberbullying tactics, your students should be able to come up with a new tactic and lay out all the ways it can be approached and resolved as a way to coach younger students so they don't have to go through the same thing. Build the pieces in this free digital storytelling application, Primary Access (www.primaryaccess.org) with photos, videos, advice, and resources. Use our framework of "Understand, Prevent, Combat, and Transform" and build in a group activity that you create yourself. When your class has finished with this project, send it to our website, Cyberslammed (www.cyberslammed.com) and we will highlight your class project for other students across the country.

Ideas And Notes

_____

_____

_____

_____

_____

_____

_____

_____

_____

_____

_____

_____

_____

_____

Appendix A
Student Survey To Determine Which Tactics To Cover

1. I have and use the following:

☐ A cell phone

☐ An email account

☐ A social networking profile (like MySpace, Facebook, Bebo, Orkut, Hi5)

☐ My own website

☐ A digital camera or a cell phone camera

☐ A video camera or a video on my cell phone

☐ An online game (Xbox, PS3, Wii)

☐ iPod with video or phone

☐ I don't use any of these

2. If you or someone you know has ever been bullied online, where did it happen?
(You can answer more than one)

☐ On MySpace, Facebook or another social networking site

☐ Email

☐ Instant Messaging (IM)

☐ A website

☐ Cell phone/texting/voicemail

☐ Message Board

☐ Chat Room

☐ In photos

☐ A blog

☐ Somebody posted an anonymous comment

☐ An online world (like World of Warcraft)

☐ Interactive game (Xbox 360 Sony PlayStation 3, Nintendo DS, and Sony PSP)

☐ None of these

Go through each one of these and tell us *how* cyberbullying has specifically happened to you or someone you know, if at all.

3. Write "Yes" if cyberbullying has specifically happened to you or someone you know. Write "No" in the box if it didn't happen.

Cyberbullying Tactic	This happened to me.	This happened to someone I know.	For Parents/Educators (Applicable Chapter)
1. Someone wrote about the way you look on an Internet website or social networking profile and other people joined in.			Digital Pile On, Rating Website, Imposter Profile, Haters' Club, Sexting
2. A private picture of yourself was "stolen" online and put on someone else's website or social networking profile.			Rating Website, Imposter Profile, Haters' Club, Sexting
3. A person or a group made a website or social networking profile about you that you didn't know about.			Rating Website, Imposter Profile, Haters' Club, Sexting, Videojacking
4. Someone started a rumor about you or ganged up on you online.			Rating Website, Haters' Club, Digital Pile On
5. Someone used your phone without you knowing to send a text as a joke to someone else.			Imposter Profile, Sexting
6. A group of people sent a bunch of nasty or mean text messages to your email address or phone.			Haters' Club, Digital Pile On, Sexting
7. You took a sexy or naked picture of yourself and it got put online by someone else without your permission.			Sexting, Rating Website, Imposter Profile
8. Someone took an embarassing cell phone picture or video clip of you and put it on his/her social profile or website without your permission.			Sexting, Videojacking
9. You took a silly cell phone picture or video clip of yourself and put it online.			Rating Website, Videojacking
10. Someone harassed you through an online game (Xbox, PS3, PSP) or online community.			Haters' Club, Digital Pile On

Appendix B
Scene Survey

We've adapted this short form from a typical Scene Survey paramedics use upon first arriving at an accident scene when it is necessary to have a practical "shorthand" system to get all the facts before making a plan or decision. Educators and school administrators can use this form on the following page when gathering information from all parties involved in a cyberbullying situation.

Interview each student and fill out testimony.

Student Name(s):_____

Date of Incident: _____

What happened? (List exactly what was said and what the bully did)

_____

_____

Who was involved? (If anonymous, who is suspected?)

_____

_____

What type of digital media did it happen through? Circle one or more
(Email, Instant Messaging, Website, Social Networking Profile, Chat Room, Cell Phone, Photo, Video, Interactive Game, Twitter, Other)

_____

_____

If it happened through more than one digital media, list each media and write down exactly what happened.

_____

_____

_____

_____

_____

When did it first happen?

_____

_____

Were there repeated incidents? When?

_____

_____

_____

_____

_____

Do you have electronic proof that can be viewed or printed out? (Do not save or forward any nude or semi-nude video!) Attach.

How has this affected the student in or out of school?

_____

_____

_____

_____

_____

Has it affected other students directly or indirectly?

_____

_____

Witnesses to the harassment:

_____

_____

What steps were immediately taken once the harassment was reported?

_____

_____

Appendix C
Establishing Group Guidelines

1. If you have not already done so, establish guidelines for class discussions. Talking about conflict can be personal, so no one will be asked to share anything they don't want to share. Also, part of resolving conflict non-violently, without fighting, is treating other people with respect. As a group, we need to be aware of how to treat each other.

2. Introduce the following guidelines for speaking and listening in class:

    *   Talk one at a time.
    *   Don't interrupt someone who is speaking.
    *   Be respectful of other people's opinions.
    *   Don't laugh or put down other people or their contributions.
    *   Respect the privacy of others. Don't gossip about what others say.
    *   Try to stay with the topic.
    *   In small group work, try to stay on task and share the work.
    *   Say "I" when you speak of yourself.
    *   When you disagree with someone, state your opinion without attacking the other person.

3. Once a list of guidelines is established, ask the class if they agree to abide by these guidelines.

(Adapted from *Conflict Resolution in the Middle School: A Curriculum and Teacher's Guide* by William J. Kreidler copyright 1997, Educators for Social Responsibility. Used with permission.)

Appendix D
School Policy

[Note to Policy Maker: This template has been pulled from sources that are notated in the Credits. An electronic adaptable copy can be found in our online Resources (www.cyber-slammed.com). This is a comprehensive policy that defines behavioral aggression, educators' roles, as well as reporting of cyberbullying incidences. Use areas relevant to your school or district, and/or add sections that may apply or that are in accordance to your state's laws.]

SCHOOL POLICY TEMPLATE
Bullying, Cyberbullying, Harassment and
Additional Relational Aggression

The [INSERT YOUR SAD#] Board (heretofore, The Board) is committed to providing a safe, positive, productive, and nurturing educational environment for all of its students. The Board encourages the promotion of positive interpersonal relations between members of the school community. Aggressive behavior, bullying, harassment, and similar acts toward a student, whether by other students, staff, or third parties is strictly prohibited and will not be tolerated. This prohibition includes physical, verbal (oral or written), electronically transmitted (cyber or high-tech), and psychological abuse. The Board will not tolerate any gestures, comments, threats, or actions, which cause or threaten to cause bodily harm or personal degradation.

This policy applies to all activities in the District, including activities on school property or while en route to or from school-sponsored activities and those occurring off school property if the student or employee is at any school-sponsored, school-approved or school-related activity or function, such as field trips or athletic events where students are under the school's control, or where an employee is engaged in school business. This policy also applies to activities that take place off-campus if the activities cause emotional distress to an individual that substantially disrupts or interferes with the operation of a school or an individual student's ability to receive an education. The Board expects students to conduct themselves in an appropriate manner for their respective levels of development, maturity, and demonstrated capabilities with a proper regard for the rights and welfare of other students and school staff, the educational purpose underlying all school activities, and the care of school facilities and equipment.

The Board believes that standards for student behavior must be set cooperatively through interaction among the students, parents/legal guardians, staff, and community members producing an atmosphere that encourages students to grow in self-discipline. The development of this atmosphere requires respect for self and others, as well as for district and community property on the part of students, staff, and community members. Since students learn by example, school administrators, faculty, staff, and volunteers will demonstrate appropriate behavior; treat others with civility and respect, and refuse to tolerate bullying or harassment. It is the intent of the [INSERT YOUR SAD#] Board to provide all students with an equitable opportunity to learn. To that end, the Board has a significant interest in providing a safe, orderly and respectful school environment that is conducive to teaching and learning. The Board also believes that promoting ethical and responsible behavior is an essential part of the school unit's educational purpose. Ethics, responsible behavior and "character" are important if a student is to leave school as a "responsible and involved citizen" as described in the Guiding Principles of Maine's system of Learning Results. Bullying interferes with the accomplishment of this goal.

Finally, the Board recognizes the well-publicized incidents of violence and threatened violence that have occurred nationally over the past several years up to the present. As research suggests a link between bullying and school violence, the Board seeks to avoid such incidents and instead take a systematic approach to bullying prevention and intervention.

It is not the Board's intent to prohibit students from expressing their ideas, including ideas that may offend the sensibilities of others, or from engaging in civil debate. However, the Board does not condone and will take action in response to conduct that interferes with students' opportunity to learn, the educational mission of the [INSERT YOUR SAD#] schools, and the operation of the schools.

Definitions

The following definitions are provided for guidance only. If a student or other individual believes there has been aggressive behavior by a student or adult that is severe or pervasive enough to create an intimidating, hostile, or offensive educational environment, regardless of whether it fits a particular definition, s/he should report it and allow the administration to determine the appropriate course of action.

1. **"Aggressive Behavior"** is defined as inappropriate conduct, whether a single isolated incident or repeated incidents that are serious enough to negatively impact a student's or employee's educational, physical, or emotional well being. This type of behavior is a form of intimidation and harassment. It includes,

but is not limited to, behaviors such as stalking, bullying/cyberbullying, intimidating, menacing, coercion, name-calling, teasing, taunting, making threats, and hazing. Aggressive behavior can occur off-campus and individuals committing such aggressive behavior may be disciplined as provided in this policy.

2. **"Bullying"** is defined as willfully and repeatedly exercising power or control over another by systematically and chronically inflicting physical hurt or psychological distress on one or more students or school employees. (i.e., repeated oppression, physical or psychological, of a less powerful individual by a more powerful individual or group). Bullying can be physical, verbal (oral or written), electronically transmitted (cyber or high-tech), psychological (e.g., emotional abuse), through attacks on the property of another, or a combination of any of these.

Examples of conduct that may constitute bullying include, but are not limited to:

a. Physical contact or injury to another person or his or her property;

b. Threats of harm to a student, to his or her possessions, or to other individuals, whether transmitted verbally, in writing, or through cyberspace;

c. Blackmail, extortion, demands for protection money, or involuntary loans or donations;

d. Non-verbal threats and/or intimidations such as use of aggressive or menacing gestures;

e. Stalking;

f. Blocking access to school property or facilities;

g. Stealing or hiding books, backpacks, or other possessions;

h. Repeated or pervasive taunting, name-calling, belittling, mocking, put-downs, or demeaning humor relating to a student's race, color, ethnicity, gender, sexual orientation, ancestry, religion, disability, or other personal characteristics, whether or not the student actually possesses them, that could reasonably be expected to result in disruption of the instructional program or operations of the schools, or that results in a hostile educational environment for the student.

3. **"Cyberbullying"** is the use of information and communication technologies such as e-mail, cell phone, pager, text messages, instant messaging (IM), personal web sites, and online personal pooling websites, whether on or off school campus, to support deliberate, repeated, and hostile behavior by an individual or group,

that is intended to threaten or harm others, or which causes emotional distress to an individual to substantially disrupt or interfere with the operation of a school or an individual student's ability to receive an education.

Examples of conduct that may constitute cyberbullying include, but are not limited to:

    a. Posting slurs or rumors or displaying any defamatory, inaccurate, disparaging, violent, abusive, profane or sexually oriented material about a student on a website or other online application;

    b. Creating any website or posting any photograph, image, video or likeness of any student, or employee without express permission of that individual and of the principal;

    c. Posting misleading or fake photographs or digital video footage of students on websites or creating fake websites or social networking profiles in the guise of posing as the target;

    d. Sending e-mail or instant messages (IM) that are mean or threatening, or so numerous as to bombard the target's email account, IM account or drive up the target's cell phone bill;

    e. Using a camera phone or digital video camera to take and send embarrassing or "Sexting" photographs of students even if students are in a consensual relationship.

4. **"Relational Aggression"** is behavior that is intended to harm someone by damaging or manipulating his or her relationships with others. Relational Aggression is not always obvious and can include physical, verbal (malicious gossip, putdowns, insults, spreading rumors, lies, telling secrets, name calling and threats to withdraw friendships), or covert (body language, eye rolling, social exclusion, ignoring) aggression.

5. **"Cyberstalking"** as defined in s. 784.048(1)(d), F.S., [INSERT YOUR STATE'S STATUTES] means to engage in a course of conduct to communicate, or to cause to be communicated, words, photos, or language by or through the use of electronic mail or electronic communication, directed at a specific person, causing substantial emotional distress to the person and serving no legitimate purpose.

6. **"Harassment"** for purposes of this policy, includes, but is not limited to, any threatening, insulting, or dehumanizing act which subjects an individual or group to unwanted, abusive behavior of a nonverbal, verbal, written, computer

generated or physical nature directed against a student or school employee that:

    a. Demeans a person;

    b. Places a student or school employee in reasonable fear of harm to his or her person or damage to his or her property;

    c. Has the effect of substantially interfering with a student's educational performance, opportunities, or benefits; or

    d. Has the effect of substantially disrupting the orderly operation of a school.

7. "Hazing" shall be defined for purposes of this policy as performing any act or coercing another, including the target, to perform any act of initiation into any class, team, or organization that causes or creates a substantial risk of causing mental or physical harm. Permission, consent, or assumption of risk by an individual subjected to hazing shall not lessen the prohibitions contained in this policy.

8. "Intimidation" includes, but is not limited to, any threat or act intended to tamper, substantially damage or interfere with another's property, cause substantial inconvenience, subject another to offensive physical contact, or inflict serious physical injury.

9. "Menacing" includes, but is not limited to, any act intended to place a school employee, student, or third party in fear of imminent serious physical injury.

10. "Harassment, intimidation" means any act that substantially interferes with a student's educational benefits, opportunities, or performance, that takes place on or off school grounds, at any school-sponsored activity, on school-provided transportation or at any official school bus stop, and that has the effect of:

    a. Physically harming a student or damaging a student's property;

    b. Knowingly placing a student in reasonable fear of physical harm to the student or damage to the student's property;

    c. Creating a hostile educational environment; or

    d. Substantially disrupting or interfering with the operation of a school or an individual student's ability to receive an education.

Bullying & Cyberbullying Prohibited

Bullying and cyberbullying as defined in this policy, is not acceptable conduct in [YOUR SAD#] schools and is prohibited. Any student who engages in conduct that constitutes bullying or cyberbullying shall be subject to disciplinary consequences up to and including suspension and expulsion. A student's behavior may also be addressed through other behavioral interventions.

Application of Policy

For the purpose of this policy, bullying does not mean mere teasing, put-downs, trading of insults, or similar interactions among friends, nor does it include expression of ideas or beliefs so long as such expression is not lewd, profane, or does not interfere with students' opportunity to learn, the instructional program, or the operations of the schools. This does not preclude teachers or school administrators from setting and enforcing rules for civility, courtesy, and/or responsible behavior in the classroom and the school environment. The determination whether particular conduct constitutes bullying requires reasonable consideration of the circumstances, which include the frequency of the behavior at issue, the location in which the behavior occurs, the ages and maturity of the students involved, the activity or context in which the conduct occurs, and the nature and severity of the conduct.

Delegation of Responsibility

The Superintendent/designee will be responsible for developing and implementing procedures for:

a. Student and parent reporting of bullying to staff and school administrators;

b. Staff reporting of bullying to school administrators;

c. Review of reports and investigation of bullying incidents;

d. Intervention with and/or discipline of students who engage in bullying;

e. Support for students who are targets of bullying;

f. Training staff and students in bullying prevention; and

g. Periodic evaluation of bullying prevention, intervention, and training efforts in [YOUR SAD#] schools and reporting to the Board upon request.

Reporting

Procedures for reporting bullying, harassment, or similar acts covered by this policy, including provisions that permit a person to anonymously report such an act, are as follows:

1. Any student who believes s/he has been or is the target of bullying, harassment, or aggressive behavior should immediately report the situation to the principal, assistant principal, or the Superintendent. The student may also report concerns to a teacher or counselor who will be responsible for notifying the appropriate administrator or Board official.

2. Every student is encouraged, and every staff member is required, to report any situation that they believe to be bullying, harassment or aggressive behavior directed toward a student. Reports by students may be made anonymously by calling SpeakOut Hotline @ 1.800.226.7733 or going online to *SchoolTipline* at http://www.schooltipline.com or by directing their report to those identified above.

3. A school employee, school volunteer, student, or parent who promptly reports in good faith an act of bullying, harassment, or similar act to the appropriate school official designated in this policy and who makes this report in compliance with the procedures set forth in this policy is immune from a cause of action for damages arising out of the reporting itself or any failure to remedy the reported incident.

4. Any written or oral reporting of an act of bullying, harassment, or similar act shall be considered an official means of reporting such act(s). Reports may be made anonymously, but formal disciplinary action may not be based solely on the basis of an anonymous report.

The prompt investigation of a report of bullying, harassment, or similar act is deemed to be a school-related activity and begins with a report of such an act. Procedures for investigation include, but are not limited to the following:

1. The principal or designee selects a designee(s), employed by the district, trained in investigative procedures to initiate the investigation (not to include the accused perpetrator or target).

2. Documented interviews of the target, alleged perpetrator, and witnesses shall be conducted privately, separately, and are confidential. Each individual (target, alleged perpetrator, and witness) will be interviewed separately and at no time will the alleged perpetrator and target be interviewed together.

The investigator shall collect and evaluate the facts including, but not limited to:

a. Description of incident(s) including nature of the behavior; context in which the alleged incident(s) occurred, etc.;

b. How often the conduct occurred;

c. Whether there were past incidents or past continuing patterns of behavior;

d. The relationship between the parties involved;

e. The characteristics of parties involved (i.e., grade, age, etc.);

f. The identity and number of individuals who participated in bullying or harassing behavior;

g. Where the alleged incident(s) occurred;

h. Whether the conduct adversely affected the student's education or educational environment;

i. Whether the alleged target felt or perceived an imbalance of power as a result of the reported incident; and

j. The date, time, and method in which the parents/legal guardians of all parties involved were contacted.

Whether a particular action or incident constitutes a violation of this policy requires a determination based on all the facts and surrounding circumstances.

The investigator shall ensure that all investigative procedural steps are completed within ten (10) school days from the initial filing of the complaint or report of bullying, harassment, or similar act.

The highest level of confidentiality possible will be upheld regarding the submission of a complaint or a report of bullying, harassment, or similar act, and the investigative procedures that follow.

A principal or designee will assign a designee(s) that is trained in investigative procedures to initiate an investigation of whether an act of bullying or harassment is within the scope of the school district.

The trained designee(s) will provide a report on results of the investigation with recommendations for the principal to make a determination if an act of bullying, harassment, or similar act, falls within the scope of the district.

1. If the alleged act is within the scope of the district, the principal will institute the district's Procedures for Investigating Bullying and/or Harassment.
2. If it the alleged act is outside the scope of the district, and determined to be a criminal act, the principal will refer the matter to the appropriate law enforcement authorities.
3. If the alleged act is outside the scope of the district, and determined not to be a criminal act, the principal will inform the parents/legal guardians of all students involved.

Responding to Bullying

In determining the appropriate response to students who engage in bullying behavior, school administrators should consider the ages and maturity of the students involved, the type of behaviors, the frequency and/or pattern of behaviors, the context in which the incident occurred, and other relevant circumstances. Consequences may range from positive behavioral interventions up to and including suspension, expulsion, and/or reports to law enforcement officials.

Dissemination of Policy

Notice of what constitutes bullying, the Board's prohibition against bullying, and the consequences for students who bully shall be communicated to students and parents through the Student Code of Conduct and Student Handbook.

STATUTORY AUTHORITY: [INSERT YOUR STATE'S STATUTES]

HISTORY
ADOPTED: [DATE]

REVISION DATE(S): [DATE]

BOARD REVIEW: [DATE]

Appendix E
Parent/Student Contract

An electronic adaptable copy can be found in our online Resources on our website Cyber-slammed (www.cyberslammed.com).

EDUCATOR AND STUDENT ACCEPTABLE USE POLICY
FOR USING TECHNOLOGY & COMPUTERS IN & OUTSIDE SCHOOL

Adapted from the Catholic Schools of the Archdiocese of Philadelphia with permission

SCOPE OF USE

School technology is to be used for educational purposes. Uses mentioned in this policy apply to **inside school** use and may, in certain instances, apply to personal technology use and/or uses **outside of school**. Where personal outside use of technology threatens a likelihood of substantial disruption in school, including harming or interfering with the rights of other students or teachers to participate fully in school or extracurricular activities, these activities may be viewed as a violation of the Acceptable Use Policy and may be subject to the disciplinary measure found herein.

Acceptable Technology Use

Students using school technology may communicate and create electronic material for educational purposes as long as they respect and protect the school's electronic property, as well as the privacy and the intellectual property of others.

Unacceptable Technology Use

Students using school technology must <u>not</u>:

- Deliberately visit a site known for unacceptable material or any material that is not in support of educational objectives; Harass, threaten, deceive, intimidate, offend, embarrass, or annoy any individual;
- Post, publish, or display any defamatory, inaccurate, violent, abusive, profane or sexually oriented material. Users must not use obscene, profane, lewd, vulgar, rude or threatening language. Users must not knowingly or recklessly post false information about any persons, students, staff or any other organization;
- Create any site or post any photograph, image, video or likeness of any student, or employee without express permission of that individual and of the principal;
- Attempt to "get around" system security;
- Violate license agreements by downloading illegal copies of music, games, or movies;
- Use technology for any illegal activity;

- Breach confidentiality obligations of school or system employees;
- Harm the goodwill and reputation of the school or system in the community;
- Transmit any material in violation of any local, federal and state laws. This includes, but is not limited to: copyrighted material, licensed material and threatening or obscene material.

Reporting Abuse: Users must immediately report any damage or change to the school's hardware/software that is noticed by the user. Users also agree to report any threats, or harassment (online and off) to school administrators.

Administrative Rights: The School has the right to monitor both student and employee use of school computers and computer accessed content. Due to the evolving nature of Technology, the School reserves the right to amend or add to this policy at any time without notice.

Policy Violations

Violation of the above rules will be dealt with by the administration of the school. Violation of these rules may result in any or all of the following:

- Loss of use of the school network, computers and software, including Internet access. The student will be expected to complete work on a non-networked, stand-alone computer system;
- Issuance of demerits/detentions, if applicable;
- Disciplinary action including, but not limited to, dismissal and/or legal action by the school, civil authorities, or other involved parties.

I UNDERSTAND AND AGREE TO FOLLOW THE ABOVE RULES:

Student Internet Access Contract

I understand that when I am using the Internet or any other computer/telecommunications device, I must adhere to all rules of courtesy, etiquette, and laws regarding the copying of information as prescribed by either Federal, State, or local laws and (School name).

My signature below and that of my parents(s) or guardian(s) signature means that I agree to follow the guidelines of this *Acceptable Use Policy for Technology*.

Student Name _____

Student Signature _____

Date _____/_____/_____

I UNDERSTAND THE ABOVE RULES AND HAVE MADE SURE MY SON/ DAUGHTER ALSO UNDERSTOOD EACH ONE BEFORE SIGNING THIS CONTRACT:

Parent or Guardian: Student Access Contract

I hereby release (School name), its personnel and any other institutions with which it is affiliated, from any and all claims and damages of any nature arising from my child's use of, or inability to use, the Internet Access, including but not limited to claims that may arise from the unauthorized use of the system to purchase products or services.

As the parent or guardian of this student, I have read the *Acceptable Use Policy for Technology* and hereby give my permission for my child to use the Internet. I understand that my child has agreed not to access inappropriate material on the Internet.

Parent/Guardian Signature _____

Date _____/_____/_____

resources

Within this workbook there are several references to more online Resources. In order to save space and to keep additional information around our six chapters fresh and current, all information listed within the text under the term "Resources" can be found on the authors' website (www.cyberslammed.com) for your convenience. The authors do not control any linked websites, which may have different privacy policies, so follow their advice under your own discretion.

We have made every effort to trace the ownership of all copyrighted material and to secure permission from copyright holders. In the event of any question arising as to the use of any material, we will be pleased to make the necessary corrections in future printings. Thanks are due to the following authors, publishers, and individuals for permission to use the material indicated:

The 5 C's are used with permission and adapted from "The 10 C's: A Model of Diversity, Awareness and Social Change," by Patti DeRosa, President, ChangeWorks Consulting: www. changeworksconsulting.org, and Dr. Ulric Johnson, Assistant Dean, School of Human Services, Springfield College, Boston, MA.

"The Bullying Circle" of the Olweus Bullying Prevention Program, Teacher Guide by Dan Olweus, Ph.D., Susan B. Limber, Ph.D, Vicki Crocker Flery Ph.D., Nancy Mullin, M.Ed., and Marlene Snyder, Ph.D., has been reprinted by permission of Hazelden Foundation, Center City, MN. Copyright 2007 by the Hazelden Foundation.

Chat Acronym List: Provided with permission from the National Center for Missing & Exploited Children. Copyright 2007. All rights reserved.

The Eight Stages of Genocide is used with permission from Dr. Gregory H. Stanton, President, Genocide Watch.

The Event Empathy Action Exercise is used with permission from David A. Levine. (www. davidalevine.com).

Excerpts adapted from *Conflict Resolution in the Middle School: A Curriculum and Teacher's Guide* by William J. Kreidler. Copyright 1997, Educators for Social Responsibility. Used with permission.

Excerpts used from *Creating the Peaceable School* (pp. 214-217) by Richard J. Bodine, Donna K. Crawford, and Fred Schrumpf (1994), Champaign, IL: Research Press. Copyright 1994 by Richard J. Bodine, Donna K. Crawford, and Fred Schrumpf. Reprinted by permission.

INTRODUCTION

1   Meier, Tina. "The Story." *The Megan Meier Foundation*, Wednesday, Jan. 24, 2009. http://www.meganmeierfoundation.org.

2   "Parents: Cyber Bullying Led to Teen's Suicide Megan Meier's Parents Now Want Measures to Protect Children Online." *ABC Good Morning America* Nov. 19, 2007. pp 1-3, Web. Sept. 9, 2009, http://abcnews.go.com/GMA/story?id=3882520&page=1.

3   "Cyberbullying Not An Epidemic . . . Not Killing Our Children." *Suicide Prevention News and Comment* July 15, 2009. Web. Jan. 24, 2011. http://suicideprevention-community.wordpress.com/2009/07/15/cyberbullying-not-an-epidemic-not-killing-our-children.

4   Khadaroo, Stacy Teicher. "Report: One-third of US teens are victims of cyber-bullying." *Christian Science Monitor* Oct. 8, 2010: pp 1-2, Web. Feb. 14, 2011. http://www.csmonitor.com/USA/Society/2010/1008/Report-One-third-of-US-teens-are-victims-of-cyberbullying.

5   "A Thin Line." AP-MTV Digital Abuse Study (August 2011): 1. Web. Oct. 3, 2011. MTV-AP_2011_Research_Study_Exec Summary.pdf

6   "A Thin Line." AP-MTV Digital Abuse Study (August 2011): 2.

7   Hinduja, Dr. Sameer and Dr. Justin W. Patchin. "Research." *Cyberbullying Research Center*. Feb. 2010, Web. Feb. 14, 2011. http://www.cyberbullying.us/research.php.

8   "A Thin Line." AP-MTV Digital Abuse Study (August 2011): 1.

9   "About MLTI." *Maine Learning Technology Initiative*. http://www.Maine.gov, n.d. Web. Jan. 24, 2011, http://maine.gov/mlti/about/index.shtml.

OVERVIEW

10   Stutzsky, Glenn. "Cyberbullying Information." *Institute for Public Policy and Social Research* March 2006 pp.1-3. Web. Feb. 14, 2011. http://www.ippsr.msu. edu/.../2006_Mar_CYBER_BULLYING_INFORMATION_2006%20--%20 Provided%20by%20Mr.%20Glenn%20Stutzky.pdf.

11   Collier, Anne. Telephone interview. Jan. 11, 2011.

12   Hinduja, Dr. Sameer and Dr. Justin W. Patchin. "Fact Sheet—Cyberbullying: Identification, Prevention, and Response." *Cyberbullying Research Center* 2010. Web. Feb. 15, 2011, http://cyberbullying.us/index.php.

13   Hinduja and Patchin, Fact Sheet, 2.

14   Willard, Nancy. Cyberbully Resources. "I Can't See You—You Can't See Me: How the Use of Information and Communication Technologies Can Impact Responsible Behavior." *Center For Safe and Responsible Internet Use.* 2004. Web. Mar. 4, 2011. http://csriu.org/cyberbully.

15   Hinduja and Patchin, Fact Sheet, 2

16   Mesch, Gustavo. "Parental Mediation, Online Activities and Cyberbullying." Gustavomesch's Blog A weblog on social media and society based on real research. Wordpress.com, Jul. 1, 2010. Web. Feb. 15, 2011.

17   Olweus, Dan. *Olweus Bullying Prevention Program, Teacher Guide.* Center City, MN: Hazelden Publishing, 2007, p 24, Print.

18   Collier, Anne. "Clicks & cliques: *Really* meaty advice for parents on cyber-bullying." *Net Family News.org.* Net Family News.org Feb. 12, 2010. Web. pars 3, 4 Feb. 15, 2011. http://www.netfamilynews.org/2010/02/clicks-cliques-really-meaty-advice-for.html.

19   Ybarra, MPH, Michele L., Kimberly J. Mitchell, PhD, David Finkelhor, PhD, and Janis Wolak, JD. "Internet Prevention Messages Targeting the Right Online Behaviors." *Archives of Pediatrics & Adolescent Medicine* Vol. 161 No. Feb. 2, 2007. par 1, Web. Feb. 15, 2011.

20   Collier, Anne. "Notes from a conference on bullying." *Net Family News.org.* Net Family News.org, Nov. 18, 2010. Web. Feb. 15, 2011.

21   Davis, Stan. "Anne Collier recommended I email you." Email to the author. Feb. 21, 2011.

22   Hirschhorn Donahue, Elisabeth, Ron Haskins, and Marisa Nightingale, "Using the Media to Promote Adolescent Well-Being," Policy Brief: Children and Electronic Media 18.1 (Spring 2008): 2, Web. Feb. 21, 2011. http://futureof-children.org/futureofchildren/publications/journals/journal_details/index.xml?journalid=32.

23   Collier, Anne. Personal interview. Jan. 11, 2011.

24   Collier, Anne. Jan. 11, 2011.

25   "Cyberbullying." *Stop Bullying Now.* U.S. Department of Health and Human Services. Web. Feb. 16, 2011. http://www.stopbullyingnow.hrsa.gov/adults/cyber-bullying.aspx.

26   *Stop Bullying Now*

27   *Stop Bullying Now*

28   Collier, Anne. "Notes from a conference on bullying."

29   Bodine, Richard J. and Donna K. Crawford. *Developing Emotional Intelligence: A Guide to Behavior Management and Conflict Resolution in Schools.* 1st, Champaign, IL: Research Press, 1999, 113, Print.

30   Bodine and Crawford, 113.

31   Collier, Anne. "Clicks, cliques & cyberbullying, Part 2: Whole-school response is key." *Net Family News.org.* Net family News.org Feb. 18, 2010, par 5, Web. Feb. 15, 2011, http://www.netfamilynews.org/labels/Rosalind%20Wiseman.html.

32   Hutton, Thomas. "Cyberslammed" cyberbullying collaborators—checking in." Email to author. Nov. 8, 2009.

33   Collier, Anne. Email to author. Feb. 2, 2011.

34   McBride, Shanterra. "Possible collaboration on cyberbullying?" Email to author. Jan. 10, 2010.

35   Hutton, Thomas. Email to author. Nov. 8, 2009.

36   Hutton, Thomas. Email to author. Nov. 8, 2009.

37   Willard, Nancy. Email to author. Jan. 20, 2011.

CHAPTER ONE: A DIGITAL PILE ON

38   "A Thin Line." AP-MTV Digital Abuse Study (September 2009): 2. Web. Feb. 25, 2011. http://www.athinline.org/MTV-AP_Digital_Abuse_Study_Executive_Summary.pdf.

39   Brinkman, Dr. Rick, and Dr. Rick Kirschner. *Dealing with People You Can't Stand: How to Bring Out The Best In People At Their Worst.* New York: McGraw-Hill, Inc., 2002. 83. Print.

40   MacDonald, Gregg. "Cyber-bullying defies traditional stereotype." *FairfaxTimes* Sept. 1, 2010: par 11, Web. Feb. 15, 2011. http://www.fairfaxtimes.com/cms/story.php?id=2078.

41   North, Anna. "The Meaning of Mean: The Death Of The Mean Girl." *Jezebel.* Gawker Media. Feb. 18, 2011. Web. Feb. 21, 2011, http://jezebel.com/#!5764513/is-the-mean-girl-dead.

42   Mikel Brown, Lyn. "Interested in providing a quote for our cyberbullying manual?" Email to author. Aug. 30, 2009.

43   Bodine and Crawford. *Developing Emotional Intelligence*, 72.

44   Bodine and Crawford. *Developing Emotional Intelligence*, 158.

45   "The Adolescent Brain: Why Teenagers Think And Act Differently." *EDinformatics:* Education for the Information Age. Web. Jan 24, 2011. http://www.edinformatics.com/news/teenage_brains.htm.

46   Girard, Kathryn and Susan J. Koch. *Conflict Resolution in the Schools*. 1st. San Francisco: Jossey-Bass, 1996, Print.

47   Girard and Koch. *Conflict Resolution in the Schools*, 61.

48   "Blocking someone." *Google Talk*. Google, Web. Jan. 25, 2011. <http://www.google.com/support/talk/bin/answer.py?hl=en&answer=23941

49   "Chat Abbreviations." *Missing Kids*. National Center For Missing and Exploited Children, 2007. Web. Mar 11, 2011.

50   Brinkman, Dr. Rick and Dr. Rick Kirschner. *Dealing with People You Can't Stand*, 83.

CHAPTER TWO: RATING WEBSITE

51   "Rating Site." *Wikipedia*. 2010. Web. http://en.wikipedia.org/wiki/Rating_site.

52   Tyler, Josh. "Read The Real Mark Zuckerberg's Original Facemash Apology From 2003." *Cinema Blend* Oct. 3, 2010: 1. Web. Jan. 25, 2011. http://www.cinemablend.com/new/Read-The-Real-Mark-Zuckerberg-s-Original-Facemash-Apology-From-2003-20965.html.

53   "Rating Site." *Wikipedia*

54   "Terms Of Service." *Rate My Body*. Web. Jan. 25, 2011. http://www.ratemybody.com/terms.aspx.

55   Bodine and Crawford, *Developing Emotional Intelligence*, 82.

56   Bodine and Crawford, *Developing Emotional Intelligence*, 86.

57   "List of emotions." *Wikipedia*. 2011. Web. http://en.wikipedia.org/wiki/List_of_emotions.

58   "Screenshot." *Wikipedia*. 2011. Web. Jan. 9, 2011 http://en.wikipedia.org/wiki/Screenshot.

59   "Google alerts." *Google*. 2011. Web. Jan. 29, 2011. http://www.google.com/alerts.

60   Henderson, Jim. "4 Ways To Watermark Your Images Online." *Makeuseof.com* Dec. 2, 2008: 1. Web. Jan 29, 2011. http://www.makeuseof.com/tag/watermarks-marking-your-image-territory.

61   Fertik, Michael, and David Thompson. *Wild West 2.0.* 1st. New York, NY: AMACOM, American Management Association, 2010. 97. Print.

62   "Privacy, editing, tagging and abuse." *Help Center.* Facebook. 2011. Web. Jan. 29, 2011. http://www.facebook.com/help/?faq=15560&ref_query=untag+photos.

63   "Terms Of Service." *Rate My Body*

64   Anonymous. "Fake Photo Online Dating Sites." *My Worst Secret.* Tres Consultantes, Dec. 4, 2010. Web. Jan. 31, 2011. http://myworstsecret.com/694

CHAPTER THREE: IMPOSTER PROFILE

65   "A Thin Line." AP-MTV Digital Abuse Study (September 2009): 2. Web. Feb. 25, 2011. http://www.athinline.org/MTV-AP_Digital_Abuse_Study_Executive_Summary.pdf.

66   Girard and Koch. *Conflict Resolution in the Schools*, 67.

67   Kreidler, William J. *Conflict in the Middle School.* Field Test Version. 1. Cambridge, MA: Educators for Social Responsibility, 1994. 26. Print.

68   Bodine and Crawford, *Developing Emotional Intelligence*, 89.

69   Chen, Adrian. "How to Keep Secrets—Even on Facebook." *Valleywag.* 13 Nov. 2010: Web. Jan. 31, 2011. http://gawker.com/5688664/how-to-keep-secretseven-on-facebook?skyline=true&s=i.

70   Arrington, Michael. "Being Eric Schmidt (On Facebook)." *TechCrunch.* Oct. 10, 2010: Web. Jan. 31, 2011. http://techcrunch.com/2010/10/10/being-eric-schmidt-on-facebook.

71   Corica, Susan. "Former Bristol Eastern students arrested for cyberbullying." *Bristol Press* Nov. 30, 2010. Web. Dec. 14, 2010. http://www.bristolpress.com/articles/2010/11/30/news/doc4cf5cf7a7fb4f769490573.txt

72   Hutton, Thomas. Email to author. Nov. 8, 2009.

73   "Cyberbullying." Stop Bullying Now. *U.S. Department of Health and Human Services.* Par 35. Web. Feb. 16, 2011. http://www.stopbullyingnow.hrsa.gov/adults/cyber-bullying.aspx.

74   Corica, Susan. "Former Bristol Eastern students arrested for cyberbullying." *Bristol Press* Nov. 30, 2010.

75   Gendreau, Leanne. "Bristol Woman Fights Back After Cyber Bullying." *NBC Connecticut* Dec. 8, 2010: 1. Web. Feb. 2, 2011. http://www.nbcconnecticut.com/news/local-beat/Bristol-Woman-Fights-Back-After-Cyber-Bullying-111520759.html.

CHAPTER FOUR: HATERS' CLUB

76   Coloroso, Barbara. *The Bully, the Bullied and the Bystander: From Preschool to High School-How Parents and Teachers Can Help Break the Cycle of Violence.* New York, NY: HarperCollins, 2003. 21. Print.

77   Stanton, Gregory H. "The 8 Stages of Genocide." *Genocide Watch: The International Campaign to End Genocide.* International Campaign to End Genocide, 1998. Web. Feb. 22, 2011. http://www.genocidewatch.org/aboutgenocide/8stagesofgenocide.html.

78   Richard J. Bodine, Donna K. Crawford, and Fred Schrumpf, qtd. in Bodine and Crawford's *Developing Emotional Intelligence, 66.*

79   DeRosa, Patti, and Ulric Johnson. "The 10 Cs A Model Of Diversity Awareness And Social Change." *Changeworks Consulting* 2002: pp 2-5. Web. Mar. 1, 2011.

80   Kreidler, William J. *Conflict in the Middle School.* 213.

81   Google alerts. http://www.google.com/alerts

82   Pollack, Alye. Dir. Words are worse than Sticks and Stones. *YouTube*: 2011, Web. Apr. 6, 2011.

83   "Westport 8th Grader Fights Bullies With YouTube Video." *CBS New York.com* March 29, 2011 Web. Apr. 6, 2011. http://newyork.cbslocal.com/2011/03/29/ westport-8th-grader-fights-bullies-with-youtube-video.

CHAPTER FIVE: SEXTING

84   Lenhart, Amanda, Rich Ling, Scott Campbell, and Kristen Purcell. "Teens and Mobile Phones." *Pew Internet & American Life Project* Apr. 20, 2010. 2. Pew Research Center. Web. Feb. 4, 2011. http://pewinternet.org/Reports/2010/ Teens-and-Mobile-Phones/Summary-of-findings/Findings.aspx?r=1.

85   Lenhart, Amanda. "Teens and Sexting: Overview and Introduction." *Pew Internet & American Life Project* Dec. 15, 2009: pars 1. Web. Feb. 25, 2011. http://www. pewinternet.org/Reports/2009/Teens-and-Sexting/Overview.aspx.

86   Mitchell, Kimberly J., David Finkelhor, Lisa M. Jones, and Janis Wolak. "Prevalence and Characteristics of Youth Sexting: A National Study." *Pediatrics*. 129.1 (2012): 1. Print.

87   Kaufman, Gil. "Cyberbullying, Sexting Widespread, MTV/AP Survey Reveals."

88   "A Thin Line." AP-MTV Digital Abuse Study (September 2009): 3.

89   "Sex and Tech." The National Campaign to Prevent Teen and Unplanned Pregnancy and CosmoGirl.com: 4.

90   "Sex and Tech." *The National Campaign to Prevent Teen and Unplanned Pregnancy and CosmoGirl.com*: 4.

91   Lenhart, Amanda, Rich Ling, Scott Campbell, and Kristen Purcell. "Teens and Mobile Phones." *Pew Internet & American Life Project*: 87.

92   Willard, Nancy, "Sexting & Youth: Achieving a Rational Response." *Center for Safe and Responsible Internet Use*, (Feb. 5, 2010): p 5, Print.

93   Willard, Nancy, "Sexting & Youth: Achieving a Rational Response." p 8.

94   McCullagh, Declan. "Police blotter: Teens prosecuted for racy photos." *CNET News* Feb. 9, 2007: n. pag, Web. Feb. 8, 2011, http://news.cnet.com/Police-blotter-Teens-prosecuted-for-racy-photos/2100-1030_3-6157857.html.

95   Hitchcock, Jayne A. "Lecture/Presentation Inquiry." Email to author. Sept. 28, 2009

96   Jayson, Sharon. "Flirting goes high-tech with racy photos shared on cell phones." *USA Today.* Dec. 9, 2008: 1, Web. Feb. 8, 2011 http://www.usatoday.com/tech/news/internetprivacy/2008-12-09-high-tech-flirting_N.htm.

97   Blackshaw, Pete. "A Pocket Guide to Social Media and Kids." *Nielsenwire* Nov. 8, 2009): 1, Web. Feb. 4, 2011, http://blog.nielsen.com/nielsenwire/consumer/a-pocket-guide-to-social-media-and-kids.

98   Girard, Kathryn and Susan J. Koch. *Conflict Resolution in the Schools* p 80.

99   Girard, Kathryn and Susan J. Koch. *Conflict Resolution in the Schools* p 80.

100   Bodine, Richard J., Donna K. Crawford, and Fred Schrumpf., *Creating the Peaceable School: A Comprehensive Program for Teaching Conflict Resolution*, pp. 214-217. 1994 Champaign, IL: Research Press.

101   "Your Stories." *A Thin Line.* MTV. Web. February 8, 2011. http://www.athinline.org/real-stories.

102   "Google alerts." *Google*

103   TigerText Secure Mobile Messaging. *TigerText.* 2011, Web. Feb. 8, 2011 http://www.tigertext.com.

104   Herman, Joshua. Telephone interview with author. March 30, 2011.

105   Hitchcock, Jayne A. "Lecture/Presentation Inquiry." Email to author. Sept. 28, 2009

106   "Sexting: What Is It?" *A Thin Line.* MTV, March 3, 2011. Web. Feb. 8, 2011. http://www.athinline.org/facts/sexting.

107   Rowland, Kara. "Sexting' is thorny legal issue." *Washington Times,* June 23, 2009: 1, Web. Feb. 24, 2011. http://www.washingtontimes.com/news/2009/jun/23/sexting-is-thorny-legal-issue.

108   "Bullying expert recommends teens delete most "sexting" messages." *Safety Village* Feb. 23, 2011: par 6, Web. Mar. 1, 2011 http://www.safetyvillage.com/2011/02/23/bullying-expert-recommends-teens-delete-most-%E2%80%9Csexting%E2%80%9D-messages.

109   Patchin, Justin. "You Received a "Sext," Now What?" *Advice for Teens blog.* Cyberbullying Research Center. Feb. 28, 2011, Web. March 1, 2011 http://cyberbullying.us/blog/you-received-a-sext-now-what-advice-for-teens.html.

110   Herman, Joshua. Telephone interview with author. March 30, 2011.

111   Seltzer, David S. "Former School Official Gets 'Nuisance Settlement' in Lawsuit Over Student Sexting." *Cyber Crime Lawyer Blog.* Seltzer Law, Nov. 15, 2010, Web. March 1, 2011. http://www.cybercrimelawyerblog.com/2010/11/former_school_official_gets_nu.html.

112   Herman, Joshua. Telephone interview with author. March 30, 2011.

113   Jones, Stephanie E. and Sara Boucek. "Sexting In Schools: Handling Student Discipline In Light Of Technology Changes." *National School Boards Association* (April 10, 2010): 4, Web. Feb. 24, 2011, Print.

114   Herman, Joshua. "Sexting: It's No Joke, It's a Crime." *Illinois Bar Journal* (April, 2010): 192, Web. Feb. 25, 2011. http://www.isba.org/ibj/2010/04/criminutesallaw#1

115   "Tips to Prevent Sexting." *Netsmartz.* National Center for Missing and Exploited Children. 2009, Web. Feb. 24, 2011. http://www.netsmartz.org/downloads/tipsheets/sexting.pdf.

116   Bowker, M.A, Art, and Michael Sullivan, J.D., "Sexting: Risky Actions and Overreactions." *FBI Law Enforcement Bulletin*. July, 2010: par 5, Web. Feb. 24, 201. http://www.fbi.gov/stats-services/publications/law-enforcement-bulletin/july-2010/sexting.

117   CNN Wire Staff. "Elizabeth Smart abductor sentenced to life in prison." *CNN* May May 25, 2011: Web. June 23, 2011. http://www.cnn.com/2011/CRIME/05/25/utah.smart.sentencing/index.html?hpt=T2.

CHAPTER SIX: VIDEOJACKING

118   "YouTube Fact Sheet." *YouTube*. Web. Feb. 9, 2011. http://www.youtube.com/t/fact_sheet.

119   Pasternack, Alex. "After Lawsuits and Therapy, Star Wars Kid is Back." *Motherboard*, June 1, 2010: 1, Web. Feb. 9, 2011. http://www.motherboard.tv/2010/6/1/after-lawsuits-and-therapy-star-wars-kid-is-back.

120   How I Got Famous on the Internetz: David After Dentist, Keyboard Cat, Mahir, Aleksey Vayner, and More at ROFLCon. Dir. Pasternack, Alex. *Motherboard*, Dell: 2010, Film, http://www.motherboard.tv/2010/5/19/how-i-got-famous-on-the-internetz-david-after-dentist-keyboard-cat-mahir-aleksey-vayner-and-more-at-roflcon.

121   Friedman, Emily. "Victim of Secret Dorm Sex Tape Posts Facebook Goodbye, Jumps to His Death." *ABC News*. Sept. 29, 2010: pp 1-2, Web. Feb. 9, 2011. http://abcnews.go.com/US/victim-secret-dorm-sex-tape-commits-suicide/story?id=11758716.

122   Cowboy, Midnight. "The Top 5 Video Streaming Websites." *Gizmo's Freeware*, Jan. 27, 2011. Web. Feb. 9, 2011. http://www.techsupportalert.com/top-5-video-streaminutesg-websites.htm.

123   Gabler, Neal. "The Greatest Show on Earth." *Newsweek*. Dec. 21, 2009: 1. Print.

124   "A Thin Line." AP-MTV Digital Abuse Study (August 2011): 2. Web. Oct. 3, 2011. MTV-AP_2011_Research_Study_Exec Summary.pdf

125   Delisio, Ellen R. "Ways To Teach Empathy Skills." *EducationWorld.* Jan. 1, 2006: 1. Web. Oct. 1, 2011. http://www.educationworld.com/a_issues/chat/chat166. shtml.

126   "Protecting Your Privacy." *YouTube Help.* YouTube, LLC, Nov. 23, 2010. Web. Feb 10, 2011.

127   "Blocking Users." *YouTube Help.* YouTube, LLC, Sept. 10, 2010. Web. Feb. 10, 2011. http://www.google.com/support/youtube/bin/answer.py?answer=56113.

128   "How do I control commenting on my videos?" *YouTube Help.* YouTube, LLC, Oct. 9, 2010. Web. Feb. 10, 2011.

129   "Harassment and Cyberbullying." *YouTube Help.* YouTube, LLC, Sept. 10, 2010. Web. Feb. 10, 2011. http://www.google.com/support/youtube/bin/answer. py?hl=en&answer=126266

130   "Harassment and Cyberbullying." *YouTube Help.*

131   "It Gets Better." *It Gets Better Project.* Web. Apr. 19, 2011. http://www.youtube. com/user/itgetsbetterproject.

132   How I Got Famous on the Internetz: *Motherboard*

133   Bershad, Jon. "Happy Ending! The Star Wars Kid is Becoming a Lawyer." *Geeko-system.* June 3, 2010: 1. Web. Feb. 10, 2011. http://www.geekosystem.com/star-wars-kid-lawyer.

CPSIA information can be obtained at www.ICGtesting.com
Printed in the USA
BVOW060012160712

295205BV00004B/5/P